Training Your Dog

TRAINING Your Dog

Diane Ashton

The Crowood Press

First published in 1992 by
The Crowood Press Ltd
Ramsbury, Marlborough
Wiltshire SN8 2HR

© Diane Ashton 1992

British Library Cataloguing in Publication Data

A catalogue record for this book is available from the British Library.

ISBN 1 85223 655 8

Picture Credits

All photographs by the author, except those on pages 7, 12 and 13, which are reproduced by kind permission of the Metropolitan Police.

Typeset by Acorn Bookwork, Salisbury, Wiltshire
Printed and bound in Great Britain by BPCC Hazell Books, Aylesbury

Contents

Acknowledgements

I should like to thank Mum and Dad for their considerable help, guidance and support given to me over the years and for their enthusiasm and practical help given so freely during the many months it has taken to complete this book. To Mum, who has typed and retyped the manuscripts without a word processor in sight, and to Dad who combed through for errors and omissions, counting every word along the way!

Special thanks are also extended to Carol Donovan and Kathy for arranging the photo sessions and to all those who came along to them, often at short notice.

Finally, I wish to express my appreciation and thanks to Honor Holmes, one of the great dog trainers, who took the time those many moons ago to motivate a twelve-year-old girl and her crossbreed on to greater things. Thank you Honor.

Introduction

The aim of this book is twofold: first, to provide dog owners or potential owners with an insight into how a dog thinks and is motivated, and to put this knowledge to practical use in training him to be an acceptable member of the family and community; second, to promote responsible dog ownership. The majority of the population either do not own a dog or actively dislike them and its wishes must be respected. It is the irresponsible

This new recruit knows no more or less than your puppy. He will grow up to be a valuable member of his family and the community. Will yours?

owner who is making it necessary for the Government and councils to introduce prohibitive laws regarding dogs, which are also affecting the responsible dog owner.

In this book, advice is given on choosing a suitable puppy in the first place, and then follows guidance on the training needed for each stage of the puppy's life with you, as and when you need it. The purpose of the training is to mould a young puppy to fit into your lifestyle, and to prevent bad habits from developing. However, if you are thinking of giving a home to an older dog, a chapter is devoted to the challenges that you may encounter in this venture, and there is a detailed problem reference section set out in alphabetical order.

In this book I have referred to the dog as 'he'. This is used as a neutral pronoun, and does not mean that I consider a male dog to be necessarily a better pet than a bitch. There are very bossy difficult bitches, very loving dogs and vice versa. In choosing a puppy, I consider it more important to be guided by the breeder who can match a puppy to you by virtue of its character, rather than its sex.

It is often said that bitches are difficult to keep because of their coming into season twice a year, but as a pet owner there is no way you should be considering breeding from her and the ideal situation is that she should be spayed after her first season. Successful dog breeding is a very complicated process and should be left to specialist breeders who know how to get it right and produce successful, sound puppies. Against male dogs it can be said that they are always roaming, looking for bitches or are always cocking their legs at every object they pass, but it is not necessary for any dog to have to behave like this: none of the service dogs or guide dogs would be seen behaving like this. All it takes is sensible training.

Introduced in Chapter 11 are some advanced exercises which you can try with your dog. They are intended as a guide only, to enable you to have more fun with your dog, and to discover what the pair of you are capable of achieving together. If you are, however, considering heading for the top obedience competitions, I would advise you to find a serious competitive club to attend. Book after book could be written about the competitive side of dog training, but you do need to be actually in the company of already successful handlers to help steer you to the very top.

My hope is that this book will enable you to have as much pleasure with your dogs as I have had with mine over the years, and if it helps prevent just one more dog being abandoned and branded a 'problem dog', then it will have been successful.

CHAPTER 1

Responsible Dog Ownership

There are many reasons, some good, some bad, why people decide to buy their first dog. Many will be joining the thousands of dog owners who derive many years of happy, fulfilling partnerships with their dogs. For too many others the venture will bring nothing but heartbreak and misery with the dog invariably coming out worst, through no fault of his own. How many failed owners will admit the fault lies with themselves, their ill-considered decision to acquire a dog in the first place, or their failure to take time learning to understand him. It is so much easier to save face by putting the blame entirely on the dog or his breed.

When you acquire a dog, you take on certain legal responsibilities to keep him under control and prevent his becoming a nuisance to other members of the community. You are responsible for him in every way for the rest of his life, not just for the appealing puppy days. You will have to care for him in sickness and health, feed him, exercise him, groom him, spend time with him and love him. He must be trained so that he can be a pleasure for you to own. A dog does not automatically become a well-behaved member of a family, it takes a considerable amount of effort and time from his owner.

There is today a serious 'dog problem', a problem not with the dogs themselves but with careless, unthinking and selfish owners. Only about 35 per cent of the population owns a dog, which means that the large majority of people do not own a dog. Some of these people are dog lovers who for one reason or another are unable actually to have their own dog, but this still leaves a large section of the population that is indifferent to or positively does not like dogs. These people have every right to have their wishes respected and consideration must be shown to them by the dog-owning public.

Anti-dog campaigns have sprung up everywhere and have gained considerable support from all quarters. If dog owners are not prepared to show consideration to others, then unfortunately, prohibitive laws have to be introduced. More and more areas of our towns and cities are becoming out of bounds to dogs and their owners, but in all honesty, is it any wonder when we see what is happening? Dogs are now banned completely from many beaches and parks, a situation brought about by irresponsible dog owners indiscriminately letting their dogs foul these public places. With the numbers of dogs increasing and open spaces decreasing, the problem was getting out of hand.

Doing the rounds of the local swing parks when my son was young, I lost count of the number of times people allowed their dogs to mess where children were playing. Dogs were allowed to cock their legs against the swings or even the benches where people were sitting. If dog owners had shown more consideration, the total bans may not have been necessary. Fortunately, certain dog organizations, notably Pro-Dogs have fought back and achieved a lot in educating people into correct management of their dogs, so much so that it is now the accepted thing to clear up after your own dog without embarrassment. Alternatively, as you will find out in later chapters, it is quite easy to teach your dog to relieve himself on command so that he can be made to go in a suitable place.

It is also a simple fact that there are too many puppies and dogs available, and for some of these there is not going to be a permanent, loving home available. If each prospective puppy buyer had to make some effort in looking for a reputable breeder, there would be far less impulse buying and indiscriminate breeding. It is all too easy to buy a puppy by walking down the high street doing the weekly shopping and being confronted by appealing puppies in pet shop windows. All the time there is a market and people continue to buy from dealers in dogs, the trade will continue, bringing with it all the consequent problems of impulse buying, and litters being produced purely for commercial profit and exploitation of certain breeds. People will put more thought into the full implications and responsibilities of dog ownership, or into careful selection of the right type of dog for their circumstances, if they have to do some initial research and make enquiries. As a responsible dog owner, buy only from a reputable breeder.

When considering whether you can cope with the responsibilities of owning a dog, there are many questions you need to ask yourself and answer truthfully. Do you want a dog purely for the pleasure of dog ownership, or is

---

Do You Really Want a Dog?

- Can you commit yourself to the responsibilities and live with the restrictions imposed by dog ownership, for perhaps the next fifteen years?

- Do you really want to exercise every day, rain or shine, winter and summer?

- Does all your family really want a dog?

- Is somebody at home during the day with the dog? He is a pack animal and must have companionship.

- If you work during the day, are you prepared to forgo drinks after work to rush home to your dog? He cannot be left day and night.

- Are your house and circumstances suitable for a dog, both now and in the foreseeable future?

- Can you afford to buy a dog from a reputable breeder?

- Can you afford the regular vet bills and the weekly food bill?

- Can you afford the kennelling fees when you go away for weekends or holidays?

- Can you give up the time needed for exercising, grooming, training and socializing your dog?

- Are you prepared for the extra housework and the fact that your house, garden and car will never again be as immaculate as they are now?

Your garden may suffer in the first few weeks. You must put enough thought into all the consequences of dog ownership.

TRAINING YOUR DOG

With careful training, dogs can be taught an amazing variety of tasks.

it for some other reason, for example, obtaining a walking burglar alarm? The only reason you should acquire a dog is for the former reason; any other advantages that may also come from dog ownership are secondary.

Dogs are pack animals and need companionship. Are you in a position to provide this? If you are working, there will be no going for a drink or a meal straight from work if you have a dog waiting at home to be let out and exercised. If you are at home all day, your dog is going to be constantly with you. Even the children go off to school or out to play with friends, but you cannot throw your dog out on the street, or shut him out in the garden for the day.

Holidays and weekends away also need catering for. Boarding kennels need booking up early, and can be an extra expense you had not budgeted for. On the subject of finances, as well as the initial cost of buying your puppy and all his associated requirements, there are the on-going costs of feeding and veterinary expenses. All dogs need to visit their vet at least once a year for vaccination and worming schedules, but the visits can become more frequent and expensive as your dog reaches old age.

Have you thought carefully about the extra work involved once you own a dog? Your house and garden and probably your car will never be the same again. As well as the obvious extra work of dealing with dog hairs, paintwork also suffers, black greasy marks appear on door frames and skirting boards. Do you really want to exercise every day? Although it will not hurt your dog to miss his walk occasionally, he will, especially if he is an active type, need exercise on a regular basis. Are you prepared to spend time training him properly and in the early months attending dog training classes to socialize him?

Only after thinking these points through with all the family are you in a position even to consider taking further steps to acquire your puppy. If you do decide to go ahead, the next

---

The Dog Owner's Code of Conduct

- Never allow your dog to foul footpaths, parks or any public place.

- Always clean up after him if accidents do occur.

- Keep your dog under control and supervision at all times.

- Always keep him on a lead and walking to heel when on a public footpath.

- Do not take your dog into food shops or other areas where dogs are banned.

- Do not allow your dog to cause a nuisance to others by making unnecessary noise.

- Never allow your dog to roam freely through crops or grazing areas.

- Never allow your dog to chase livestock, other pets or wildlife.

- Always keep your dog regularly wormed and healthy.

- Respect the views of all sections of the community.

chapters will help you to get the right puppy to suit all your requirements, and give you an insight into how he thinks and behaves to enable you to train him correctly and get the most pleasure from your years together.

Dog and man have co-operated for generations to perform many tasks together. Dogs have shown that with careful management and training they can provide valuable assistance in various areas of our society: there are police dogs, guide dogs for the blind, search and rescue dogs and, more recently, hearing dogs for the deaf. In our homes, they can provide protection and warm companionship. I hope you will follow this book through to the end, so that your dog can provide this, and much, much more.

CHAPTER 2

Understanding your Dog

The Communication Barrier

Having made the decision to become a dog owner, you want him to become a dog of whom you can be proud, but how are you going to achieve this. You are bringing him into your home and society, into an environment with very different values and priorities to his own. If his views do not coincide with yours as he reaches adolescence, you cannot sit him down for a little heart-to-heart chat. How do you explain to him the behaviour you expect in company, the social etiquette you require when visiting the homes of friends? If he does not speak English and you cannot understand 'dog' where on earth do you start?

Some people seem to have the problem solved, and they and their dogs really do appear to understand each other. There seems to be such a bond between them that they can anticipate each other's moves and thoughts. This is the ideal situation that every aspiring dog owner hopes for. However, much as some owners would love to believe that their dog really does understand every word they say, this is just not the case. It is an impossibility, as the scientific evidence shows that his brain is not sufficiently developed to be able to differentiate between more than just a few words. What these owners do have, however, is either a natural or, in most cases, an acquired insight into dog behaviour patterns. From this, they can ensure that they have the right attitude towards their particular dog, which will allow an understanding and, therefore, a communication line to be established. If this is combined with having the right breed and type of dog to suit your personality and circumstances, you will then have the basis for many, many years of pleasure with your dog.

The Dog's Language

As humans, we communicate and learn by means of a sophisticated verbal and written language enabling us to lay down our rules for society, laws by which we all have to abide. Dogs have also evolved a communication system, not the same as ours, but nevertheless equally as complex and successful. Theirs is based on highly developed body language, a series of facial expressions, body movements and postures. The end result is the same: dogs in the wild with no human interference have a social society with strict laws in force. It has to be said that the individual members of this dog society are far better at adhering to their rules than we are to ours. They have to be, as their very existence depends upon it. The fact that these individual members are so conditioned to obey, is a great advantage to us when it comes to training dogs. If we can, therefore, begin to have some insight into how dogs communicate between themselves, and how they think and operate, our problems are half-way solved.

A dog is a very simple animal. He does not have to deal with any of our complicated human values such as good and evil, love and hate, fairness and injustice. He makes no moral judgements and is not capable of thinking in advance, of planning treachery or deceit. He has qualities that we admire and find so lacking in ourselves: loyalty to his family come what may, the ability not to hold grudges or prolong arguments. It is essential that he holds these qualities to survive, and to understand this we need to look at how the domesticated dog's ancestors operated and survived in the wild.

Dogs are descended from wolves, the most successful of the pack animals. A pack is a group of individuals operating together as a single unit, and with a well-ordered social scale. Every dog knows his position and duties on the scale and, for most of the time, is happy to accept his role in life.

The members of the pack work together, finding and killing their food and operating a defence system which offers a high degree of protection and security for each of the individual members. The individual's position on the scale determines where he sleeps, when he eats, whether he has the best of the kill or the leftovers, and he makes no major decisions in his life. His whole character is influenced by the other pack members. This is the secret of the success of the pack system. If every dog knows his position on the scale, he knows from whom he has to take orders. Constant infighting within the ranks would only weaken the pack as a whole, leading to physical injury and subsequent infection, and also to individuals becoming preoccupied with their own problems and less aware of outside predators and conditions.

Packs where the scale breaks down are soon eradicated. Every time two dogs meet, each one has to know if the other is subordinate to or superior to himself. This would be apparent by the body language and posture of each dog. The subordinate dog would adopt a submissive attitude, would creep to the superior dog and roll over on his back exposing the most

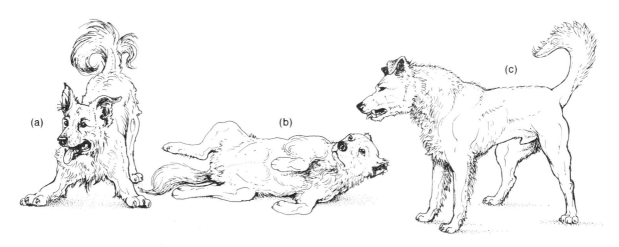

The body language of the dog. (a) Play request. The dog crouches down on his front legs, hindquarters in the air, tail waving, inviting the other dog to chase or play. (b) Submission. The dog lies on his back, exposing the soft parts of his belly. The ears are pressed back against the head. (c) A dominant aggressive stance. The dog stands stiff with straight rigid legs and hackles raised to give the impression of greater height and size. The ears are erect and forward, the head high and tail up.

Facial expressions. (a) Aggression. The lips are drawn back and the teeth bared. (b) A submissive 'grin'. The ears are laid back against the head and the mouth is closed but draws back into a sheepish grin.

vulnerable parts of his body. When this attitude is adopted, it is not necessary for the superior dog to injure the other dog. The only time any fight might occur is when two dogs meet and consider themselves to be equal. The pack system cannot operate with equals and so one would need to establish his dominance over the other. These disputes are usually dealt with swiftly and there are no major injuries inflicted. Once a dog knows he is beaten, he adopts a submissive attitude towards the victor, who will then back off. Every time these two dogs meet again, each knows his position and role in respect to the other.

At the head of every group, there has to be a leader in order to give the unit direction, and this is always the most dominant dog of the group, usually a male, but not necessarily so. This dog is known as the alpha individual or pack leader. He is the dog to whom all the others show deference. He is obeyed by everyone without question. His whole presence and demeanour demands respect and he certainly receives it. The others will always move out of his way as he passes, and he sleeps where he wants, in the best places, always on a higher level than the rest of the pack, looking down over them and the surroundings and keeping a lookout over his pack and his territory.

He always eats first, of the best, and is therefore in the best physical condition. He will ignore or demand attention from the rest of the pack as and when he wants, always on his own terms. He is the strongest, fittest, most mentally alert, and capable of being the most aggressive. He had to be to gain his position and also to maintain it against any bids to take over from lower, ambitious types. He leads the pack, makes its decisions and is aggressive to strangers within his pack's territory. He is, therefore, possessive and he takes orders from no one.

Establishing roles. The dominant dog stands erect and stiff. A submissive dog will approach a more dominant dog in a crouching position, ears back, head down, tail between his legs, everything to make himself look smaller and less threatening. He may even roll on his back and expose his belly to the dominant dog, the ultimate sign of submission.

This is the lifestyle of the ancestors of our domestic dog, and indeed of wild dogs today. It is this conditioning, enforced over many thousands of years, that we can use to our advantage in training our dogs today. Although domesticated for many thousands of years, our family dog is not that far removed from his ancestors. How often do you read of stray dogs forming packs and terrorizing neighbourhoods? How many bitches with their first litters need to be shown how to deliver and care for their offspring? Ask the owners of several dogs if the pack hierarchy still exists.

Your Family Pack

Your dog sees your family as a pack; he is incapable of thinking anything else. There-fore, it is easy to see that if you can establish yourself as pack leader, your own unit is going to live in harmony because your dog will be happy to accept and obey orders and, consequently, be easy to train.

Your Role as Pack Leader

Evolution has already programmed your dog's mind so that it is perfectly natural for him to accept and obey orders from any animal in his pack that he considers superior. However, this is the crux of the matter: *he* must consider you to be his superior. We have no direct lines of communication open to us. We cannot just tell him that he is in the subordinate role, we cannot reason with him. It is our attitude and actions towards him that will establish this.

Our own values dictate that we all try to live in equal partnerships, especially in these

19

liberated days. This, however, brings about one of the major conflicts that our dog encounters in trying to live in our society. It is a principle alien to his instincts and in this situation he would have to try and establish his own dominance. This would of course be unacceptable to us. We must therefore establish a hierarchy and the dog must be subordinate. This does not mean that we have to be aggressive or overbearing to him, but he will only be content and happy in our homes once a ranking order has been established. It is also clear that *all* humans must be of superior rank to any dog.

Leadership is established by your attitude towards your dog before any formal type of training ever starts. It is why some people are natural dog trainers without realizing it, and will always have obedient and well-mannered dogs, without the necessity of having as a last resort to rely on harsh, physical punishment.

Your role as leader is easy to establish from the time you first pick up your puppy to bring him home, and the first few days and weeks are the most important time you will ever have with your dog.

Provided you are buying your puppy at the right age from a reputable breeder, you are taking possession of not just a new addition to your family, but of an individual already used to accepting a subordinate role in life. Every litter of puppies is a pack, with the mother as the pack leader. Although a puppy may be the most dominant in the litter, he is still subordinate to his mother. It should, therefore, be an easy matter for you to take over the role of leader. Leadership, once established, is not often challenged, and if it is, it is easily dealt with. The majority of problems that occur are not because of so called 'problem dogs' but because the hierarchy in the human/dog pack has broken down.

At this stage it is worth looking to see how what should be an easy process of transferring leadership can so easily go wrong. The puppy's mother has already done most of the work for us in delivering and raising a subordinate individual. You only need to watch a litter of puppies with their mother. She will play with them and teach them, but there are certain things she will not tolerate, and she will swiftly and sharply let them know when they overstep the mark. They may run off crying, but only for a few seconds. They will come straight back to her with no resentment, happy to play again, but they will not cross her again on that particular point.

However, we can straight away lose this advantage by unintentionally putting ourselves in the subordinate position and promoting our dogs to the leader's role. Think of the following seemingly quite innocent situations. Do you allow your dog on your furniture, or even to sleep on your bed? (Who in the pack sleeps in the best places, usually the highest places? Who normally has a choice of where he sleeps?) When you open the door who passes through first, you or your dog? (Who usually goes first in the pack?) If your dog is asleep on a route through your house, in a doorway or in front of the fire, do you walk round him or make him move? Do you try not to disturb him? (Who is usually afforded this privilege in the pack?) If you are sitting reading or watching television, and your dog pushes and nudges you for a fuss, the chances are that you respond. You feel privileged that he has come to ask you. (Who in the pack normally demands and gets attention when he wants it?) If your dog agitates to go out or looks for his dinner, do you jump up immediately?

Looking at these situations, it is clear that in every case you are putting the dog in the dominant role. It can now be seen why the doting owner, running around after his dog's every whim, often says the dog loves others in the house more. The dog in fact loves no one in the way we understand the word. His version of love is respect. He has no respect for the fawning owner, as he is dominant to him, but he will respect the person who ousts him off the settee, not cruelly, but just shows him some discipline.

Leadership and the Larger Dog

The above situations do not necessarily give cause for concern with a submissive type, or even a dominant small dog. The submissive dog is quite happy to accept the privileges and the easy life, and does not have the ambition to make any further demands. But visualize what can happen with a dominant, powerful, large breed. By being promoted to leader, he will act as one and will automatically take on all the other duties associated with it. He will expect to lead the pack, so he will not be able to accept and obey commands given by subordinates. He will guard the pack and be possessive over his territory and pack (family) members. He will be aggressive over his food and possessions, it is his right to be so.

Here then, is the start of the headline-making stories. Is this dog a 'problem dog'. He was not to start with, but we now very definitely have a problem situation. All he is doing, though, is carrying out the duties that we have indicated to him so clearly in his own language that we wish him to adopt. He is exhibiting the qualities that we admire so much, loyalty (to his pack), and duty and courage in defending his pack. He is not necessarily an aggressive dog, but will use aggression if needs be to carry out his role. Modern, quality dog foods have kept him in the peak of physical condition. He is the alpha in every respect. In the dog pack he is the ultimate, the best the pack could possibly wish for. But it is totally unacceptable for him to hold this position in our society.

Assessing Your Dog's Temperament

Submissiveness and dominance are terms to describe character types, and are not to be confused with nervousness and aggression which are serious character faults to be avoided at all costs.

A dominant dog is not necessarily an aggressive dog, just as a submissive dog is not necessarily nervous.

Dominant Dogs

- More demanding to live with.

- More likely to cause problems.

- Inclined to pull on lead.

- Must *never ever* be taught, or encouraged to be aggressive.

- Must have lots of mental stimulation, or can become bored and destructive.

- Best suited to experienced trainers – for competition or as working purposes.

- Needs regular training sessions.

Submissive Dogs

- Usually make few demands.

- Generally quieter and more manageable.

- Mistakes in training easily rectified.

- Placid, laid back and less boisterous in nature.

- Excellent family pets and companions.

- Can accept missing the occasional walk and does not usually require regular training sessions.

How then could this situation have been avoided? A better approach would have been not to let your puppy get on the furniture to start with, until your respective roles have been established. You can then at a later date, allow him on the furniture, if you so wish. The difference now is that *you* are granting him this privilege. It is not his right, and you are still in the commanding position. Occasionally make the dog move if he is in your way. Always make him earn his food by making him sit for it. He will then know he has no automatic right to it. You are allowing him to have food, when you want him to have it. Do not let him push through the door before you. Occasionally, when he comes up for a fuss, make him lie down; ignore him. Just by adopting these simple attitudes you are cultivating a personality that will be biddable and easy to train.

The aforementioned changes have not been cruel, hurtful or harmful to your dog. What can be, though, are the aggressive show-downs and battles of strength that can ensue as the only means of trying to dominate a dog by sheer physical strength, especially with a dog who has already held the supreme position. A dog in this situation is confused, unhappy and unreliable, through no real fault of his own. By adopting the right attitude from the beginning, you will have a dog that is happy, obedient and willing to learn, and the formal training has not even started yet.

CHAPTER 3

The Right Dog for You

If your dog and his requirements become tedious, troublesome and unpleasurable, you are not going to be in the right frame of mind to train him successfully. It will not be his fault that you have chosen a completely unsuitable breed for your lifestyle, but inevitably it will be him that suffers in the end, and takes the blame for the consequences. The puppy you acquire is going to be part of your family for perhaps the next fifteen years, so it is worth putting in some time and thought to make sure you find the right one.

There are two things to be considered before actually buying your puppy. First, you need a dog who will be compatible with you and fulfil your needs both now and in the foreseeable future. Second, it is important to start with a puppy who is sound both in health and mind, with no major character faults to overcome.

Choosing Your Breed

There are three main areas that require careful thought at this stage: the amount of time you will be able to spend on your dog, your family circumstances and character, and finally your reasons for wanting a dog.

The amount of time you need to spend on your dog is mainly influenced by his size and his coat type. In very general terms, a larger dog needs more exercise than a smaller one, although this can be affected by a dog's own personality. Owning a large dog will also place a great deal more responsibility on you to spend more of your time ensuring that he is trained and socialized correctly. The consequences of having an out-of-control, large, powerful dog can be enormous both for your own family and others.

Coat type is a major consideration when choosing a suitable breed. Your house, garden and car can never again be as immaculate as they were prior to the arrival of your dog, but the larger and hairier he is, the greater the problem will be. Taking on a dog that you know requires frequent or specialized grooming and then subsequently ignoring or putting this fact aside, is irresponsible and leads to a

Terriers

The name terrier comes from the Latin 'Terra' meaning earth, and most terriers were originally used to chase and drive badgers, foxes and similar animals to earth, and then dig them out to kill them. Therefore, most terriers are, by nature, sturdy, courageous, pugnacious, aggressive types. They need very firm training and they can then make happy, lively and affectionate pets with a lot of character. The wire-haired terriers need frequent grooming and specialized stripping about twice a year.

Breeds include: West Highland White, Jack Russell, Bull, Staffordshire Bull, Fox (Smooth and Wire-Haired), Cairn and Airedale.

Hounds are hunters of prey and are divided into two types, scent-hounds and sight-hounds.

The scent-hound hunts with his nose to the ground, following the trail left by the prey. The hound will continually bark or 'bay' while working to enable the following sportsmen to locate his position.

The sight-hound does not use his nose, but his eyes, and he only operates when he can actually see his prey. The hound usually accompanies the huntsman with his horse, and is only unleashed when the prey is in sight. The chase is usually short and swift, with the hound overtaking the prey and pulling it down.

Hounds are of a gentle nature, very affectionate to their families but aloof to others. They can still maintain the independent streak they needed to be able to perform their original jobs efficiently and are inclined to range freely a long distance from you when running in open spaces.

Breeds include: Foxhound, Bassett, Beagle, Bloodhound, Dachshund, Afghan, Borzoi, Deerhound, Greyhound, Saluki and Wolfhound.

great deal of suffering for the dog. There are three main coat types to consider: smooth short-haired, long-haired and the wiry or non-shedding type such as that found in terriers and poodles.

The smooth short-haired type is the easiest to manage, just a quick brush over each day is all that is required and no real harm will be done if it is forgotten a few times. There is still a heavy moult to contend with, usually twice a year, and the short spiky hairs can be difficult to remove from carpets and clothing, as they seem to penetrate the fibres of the material.

Some breeds, traditionally thought of as short-haired, can cause quite a shock when they moult. These are the dogs with a double coat, an example being the German Shepherd Dog. Their coat consists of a top coat and a thick, woolly undercoat. The beginning of the moult is when the undercoat starts coming out in great tufts and you really wonder where it all comes from. The top coat is easier to deal with, but a good deal of time and effort is needed during the moult to provide extra grooming to keep your dog, and indeed your home, looking half-way presentable.

The silky long-haired coat needs a lot of attention all year. If done regularly, it need not actually take too long each day to keep this sort of coat looking glamorous. The problems start if the coat is allowed to start tangling, and this can happen after only a couple of days of being ignored. If action is not taken at this stage, the coat becomes badly matted and will eventually have to be clipped out professionally. The poor dog can become unpleasant to live with as the coat becomes smelly and unpleasant to stroke, he is uncomfortable, unhappy and spends most of his day scratching.

Toy Dogs

Dogs in this group are included purely for their size and there is therefore, a wide variety of types and characters. People unable to keep larger dogs may well find their favourite breed, or one very similar, in miniature.

Unfortunately, a lot of these dogs are not allowed to show their full potential as they are very often turned into pampered, cossetted lap dogs. However, if treated sensibly, they are as much fun and have as much spirit as their larger cousins. They make excellent companions for the elderly or disabled, but care should be taken in introducing them to a rumbustious home full of children. The dogs will love joining in with the fun and games, but with the very tiny breeds, it is easy for them to get trodden on or injured.

Breeds include: Yorkshire Terrier, Bichon Frise, Cavalier King Charles Spaniel, Chihuahua, Italian Greyhound, English Toy Terrier, Maltese, Papillon, Pekingese, Pomeranian and Pug.

Utility Dogs

This group includes breeds that do not easily fit the criteria for the other groups. Many of the breeds in this group used to be hunters, working or guard dogs, but are nowadays mainly used as pets and companions, the jobs they were bred for becoming obsolete.

They are usually fine family pets, although the group differs widely in type and character.

Breeds include: Bulldog, Chow Chow, Dalmatian, Spitz, Poodle, Lhasa Apso, Keeshund, Schnauzer and Shih Tzu.

The coat that is not shed at all may sound the ideal solution, but is in reality no easy option. These coats are very dense and get matted very quickly if not combed through thoroughly on a regular basis. The problem is that because of the sheer density of the coat, it is very easy just to go through the top layer only. When the matted coat gets wet the problem is further aggravated as it becomes literally like a layer of felt, with absolutely no chance of being combed through.

Dogs with a non-shedding coat and the wire-haired terrier breeds, require specialized grooming, usually every six to eight weeks for poodles and twice a year for terriers. This means a visit to their 'hairdresser', the canine beautician, for bathing, clipping or trimming. Will you be able to fit in these visits during your hectic schedule, or will it become another tedious chore? You could learn to clip him yourself, but this involves time and expense to learn the techniques and acquire the necessary equipment. A word of advice before you embark on this: take a look at a bathroom after a dog bathing session!

Your family circumstances and character is the next area for consideration. Are you living in a spacious house with a lot of ground, or a small flat without a garden? The latter need not necessarily preclude you from owning a larger dog, but you will need to be careful about the breed you choose. A very active, fast-moving Border Collie might become a nuisance darting about in a small confined space, and you could find one of the giant breeds always under your feet, although they are generally very laid back in nature and slow moving. One of the more placid, medium-sized breeds would probably be quite content, provided you are prepared to discipline yourself to taking him out regularly.

The character of your family is also important, and needs matching to a dog of suitable personality to fit in with you. If your dog is to play an active part of a rumbustious, lively family with children, he needs to be mentally and physically capable of joining in the fun. A dainty, delicate breed, or one with a naturally quiet nature, might not be very happy at all.

Working Dogs

This is the largest group, and it consists of guarding, herding and shepherd dogs. They have served many useful functions over the years, including police and army work, protecting flocks from predators, shepherding, rescue work, acting as guards and watchdogs. Some of the breeds can become one-man dogs and need careful training to fit into the domestic home. However, if they receive this, they make superb companions and friends. All the working breeds are highly intelligent, so they need mental as well as physical exercise; if deprived of this stimulation, they can become frustrated, destructive and unhappy.

The guarding breeds are very powerful and should never ever be taught or encouraged to be aggressive.

Breeds include: German Shepherd Dog, Collie (Bearded, Rough and Border), Old English Sheepdog, Boxer, Dobermann, Rottweiler, Great Dane, Mastiff, St Bernard, Shetland Sheepdog and Corgi.

Neither would you be content with a dog that is prone to getting over-excited with the consequent yapping associated with it. If you are elderly or infirm, and want a dog for companionship, a working breed needing a lot of mental as well as physical exercise could be a disastrous acquisition for you.

Finally, put some thought into your reasons for wanting a dog in the first place and whether your requirements might change in the future. Make sure the breed you choose will be suitable if you have a definite purpose in mind. Maybe you have watched the top-class obedience and agility competitions and are thinking you might like to take it up as a new hobby. Although you can have a good deal of success in the lower classes with almost any breed, to reach the very top in these highly competitive sports you require a dog with a lot of suppleness, agility and a will to learn and to work. It is very much a horses for courses situation, just as a carthorse would not win the Derby, there are breeds that are unlikely to become the Cruft's Obedience Champion.

The most successful dogs competing in these fields are the Border Collies, German Shepherds and retriever breeds, with many of the other working breeds doing well: Dobermanns, Rottweilers and Shelties. If you are thinking of taking up shooting, then you obviously need one of the gun-dog breeds. Hobbies can become very addictive and time-consuming, and it would be a great shame if your dog partner did not have the ability to enjoy it with you. The danger is that you could become disappointed with him and feel forced into acquiring more dogs that you are not really in a position to accommodate. Remember, a dog is for life, not to be discarded when your requirements alter.

Now you have an idea of the type of dog you need, draw up a short list of the particular breeds that attract you and that would be suitable. There are several places where you can find out more about the character and

Gundogs

Gundogs evolved from hounds and are used to hunt, point and retrieve birds. There are several specialized areas the gundogs have been bred for: pointers and setters locate the game by free-ranging large areas of the ground, retrievers collect (retrieve) the game when it falls to the ground and spaniels flush the game but are good all-rounders.

All the gundogs make excellent gentle, loving and faithful companions. The retrievers are the easiest to train. The setters are inclined to free-range when let loose and the spaniels can be extremely energetic, busy dogs.

Breeds include: Pointer (German, Short-Haired), Vizsla, Retriever (Golden, Flat-Coated, Curly-Coated, Labrador), Setter (English, Golden, Irish), Spaniel (Cocker, Clumber, Springer, Field), Weimaraner.

requirements of each breed. One is to visit a large All-Breed Show. These are advertised in the weekly dog papers *Our Dogs* or *Dog World*, which are available through newsagents.

At these shows you will certainly see the visual qualities of the various breeds, but bear in mind you are seeing them presented in the very best of condition. Try to imagine them after a long muddy walk. The show dogs are very used to the show routine, and will therefore appear extremely well behaved. They will be owned and trained by experienced dog handlers, experts in their own particular breed and with many years' experience in dealing with that breed's own peculiarities. A lot of time at dog shows is spent waiting between classes and, during a quiet period, owners will welcome the chance to discuss their dogs with you. There is a lot you can learn about the general characteristics and histories of the breeds.

Before making a final decision, take some time out to visit your local pet training club.

Your vet or police station should have the details of several in your area. This can prove to be a real eye-opener, as here you will see inexperienced dog owners facing up to problems you might never have envisaged. You will see dogs completely mismatched to their owners and home surroundings, and see all the frustration and chaos this can cause. Try to talk to people who own the breed you are considering acquiring. See if there are any particular things they are struggling with; it may be there is a common theme running through the accounts that several people give you regarding a particular breed. These are people and dogs in pet situations, and it is better to find out now if a breed might prove unsuitable. The park is also a good place to see dogs and talk to their owners. You might also meet people here who may have their second or third dog and will perhaps be able to give advice on good local breeders to approach, or bad ones to avoid.

Where to Buy your Puppy

A dog's character is known to be 40 per cent inherited and 60 per cent environment related, so as well as knowing something of the puppy's parentage, it is also important to know how the puppy has been raised since birth. Puppies start learning and being influenced by their surroundings at the age of three weeks and good or bad experiences at this age can have a dramatic and lasting effect on the adult dog. It is important that as well as interacting and learning from his own kind via his mother and his litter-mates, a puppy is also socialized with people from about the age of three weeks. Puppies deprived of this can grow up being wary of either people or dogs, which will necessitate more thought being put into their training once in your hands. Bad experiences at this young age could also give an otherwise sound and well-balanced puppy the start of a

nervous or aggressive disposition, and these are two traits the novice dog owner must avoid at all costs.

The majority of dogs still adhere very strictly to the rules of the pack, and their behaviour is predictable in differing situations. With an aggressive or nervous dog, these rules are overridden and these dogs can become very unpredictable and a liability. They need careful and experienced trainers. Never ever buy a puppy on impulse or from a pet shop or any source other than directly from the puppy's breeder. There are just too many unknowns for these acquisitions to prove consistently successful, and dog ownership is too big a commitment for a hit and miss arrangement to exist. You will have no idea of the puppy's parentage and hereditary traits and, more importantly, you will not know how the puppy has been brought up.

You will not know whether such a puppy has been socialized properly or has been brought up in a shed or, worse, come from one of the dreaded puppy farms. These 'farms' keep bitches in dark, often damp, dirty sheds, having litters every six months, each litter becoming progressively weaker as the bitch is over-producing without any extra care being given to her. These mass-produced puppies are then sent off to the pet shops for unsuspecting new owners to buy. Such puppies could well incur veterinary bills throughout their lives: a weak puppy from an ailing dam will always be a sickly adult, prone to any illness currently doing the rounds. Do not be fooled by the pedigree. It could show many champions several generations back, but if your puppy's life started off like this, it will bear little relevance. Not all pet shops are supplied by puppy farms, but a puppy that has changed hands several times, from breeder to pet shop or dealer to you, is not having the best start in life. Each change is stressful for the puppy both mentally and physically, weakening his natural defence systems.

What to Look For When Buying a Puppy

Choosing a Breeder

- How did you hear of the breeder? Personal recommendation is always the best.

- Check the puppies are being brought up in a clean environment.

- Make sure the breeder is taking care to socialize the puppies with people and introduce them to household noises. The puppies should be getting plenty of human contact.

- Make sure both parents have been screened for any inherited diseases prevalent in that breed – ask to see the certificates.

- The breeder should cross-examine you as to your suitability to have one of his puppies – it shows he cares and is not breeding for financial gain.

- Make sure you see the mother of the puppies and that she is neither nervous or aggressive. If possible, see the sire too.

- Never, every buy a puppy on impulse or from a dealer. Only ever buy a puppy directly from his breeder.

Choosing a Puppy

- Look for a healthy puppy with bright eyes and clean nose and ears. He must be nicely rounded but not pot-bellied, with loose, healthy skin and clean coat.

- Choose a puppy who is inquisitive, runs happily to you to be picked up and is not frightened by sudden noises or movements – drop your keys or similar jangly objects to check their reactions.

- Avoid a puppy that appears nervous and hides in a corner.

- Avoid a puppy that shows resentment or aggression in any way, other than normal puppy high spirits.

- Avoid the most dominant puppy in a litter – the breeder will know who he or she is.

Never buy a puppy from somebody who has just bred from a bitch they own because 'I thought it would be nice because she is so good natured'. Maybe she is of good temperament, but is she typical of her line or is she a one-off? Maybe the rest of her family are very different and this is what could then be reproduced. Does the sire's pedigree match and complement her own, or is it doubling up on specific faults? Successful dog breeding is a very complicated business, and you are better going to someone who has taken care in studying every aspect of the process to provide you with a sound stable puppy.

The best and only place to buy a puppy is directly from a caring, specialist breeder. But how do you find one in your area, and how will you know you have found one? As with anything else, personal recommendation is always to be valued, and you may already have been given the name of somebody breeding the occasional litter locally. If, when you approach this person, he has a waiting list, so much the better. A few months' wait will be worth it. It shows this person is not overbreeding for financial gain, and that their puppies already have such a good reputation that others are prepared to wait.

When you do go to view puppies, take careful note of how they are being reared. It is known that the ideal upbringing for a potential family pet is in the home from birth. They are then brought up with the hustle and bustle of home life, the comings and goings, television noises, vacuums and washing machines. Their move into your home will not then prove to be a traumatic frightening experience. However, raising a litter of puppies indoors is an extremely messy business, and not all otherwise caring breeders, are in a position to be able to do this. Provided the accommodation outside is of good quality and the breeder has been at pains to socialize the puppies with people, children, noises, and so on, and has spent time with the puppies, this should not prove to be a problem.

Choosing the Right Puppy

A breeder who has spent a lot of time with the litter will know the different characters within it, he will know who the leader is, the trouble-maker, the lazy one, the quiet one. Unless you are very confident of your dog-training abilities, tell them you do not want a dominant, pushy pup. You will be far safer having one of the others. Leave the pushy one to the experienced trainer. Although you do not want the dominant puppy, you most certainly do not want a shy or nervous one either. Avoid a puppy who seems wary of coming to see you or who huddles in a corner. Puppies from the age of four weeks should be happy running up to you inquisitively. They should be pleased to be picked up without panicking, and without

showing any aggressive tendencies. Throw down your bunch of keys and the puppies should not cower or be frightened by the noise. Look for a puppy who will go up and investigate different situations.

Do not be upset if you are interrogated by the breeder; it shows that he really cares about matching the right puppy to you, and about his puppy's future. Be truthful about your circumstances and take the breeder's advice.

If you do not know of a small, personally recommended breeder, then approach one of the larger professional breeders or show kennels. Their names can be found in the dog papers, or a list is available from the Kennel Club.

Make sure you see the mother of the pups. If there are any excuses given as to why you cannot see her, then the advice must be not to take one of the puppies. Ideally you should be able to see both parents to see that they are of good temperament. Remember that a good proportion of your puppy's character is inherited. It is not always practically possible to see the father as he may be a stud-dog living many miles away, but there should be no reason why you should not see the mother. Although a bitch may be over-protective to her pups when they are a few days old, by the time they are four weeks old she should not be showing any aggressive tendencies.

Equally, she should be willing to greet you without any signs of nervousness. If the mother is a well-balanced individual, the puppies will have been taught well by her, and been shown that humans are acceptable and welcome friends, not creatures to be feared.

A puppy that has a bad start in life health wise will grow up to be a weak adult, prone to illness and the consequent continual vet bills, so you need to look for a healthy puppy. The points to look for are alertness and liveliness; a clean coat, free from parasites or fleas (constant scratching could indicate that these are present); there should be no discharge from

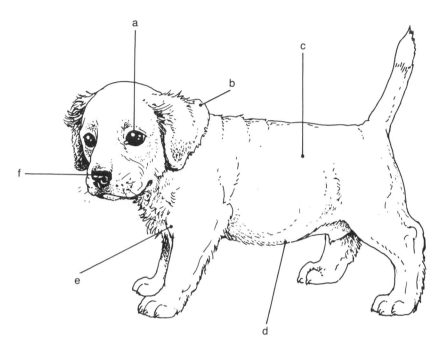

A healthy puppy. (a) The eyes should be shiny, alert and show no signs of discharge or running. (b) Ears should be clean and free from discharge or offensive odour. (c) The body should be plumpish and covered in loose folds of skin. (d) The tummy should be nicely rounded, but not pot-bellied with taut skin – a sure sign of worms. (e) The coat should be clean and shiny with no signs of parasites. (f) The nose should be cool and moist and free from discharge.

his eyes or ears, and both should look clean; his body should be nicely rounded and plumpish (if he is pot-bellied and his skin is taut, this is a sure sign that he has not been wormed properly and is not obtaining the full nourishment from his food to give him the best start in life).

Finally, in researching your chosen breed, you will have become aware of any hereditary diseases prevalent in that breed. The most common are hip dysplasia (a malformation of the hip joint causing loss of use of the hind legs), progressive retinal atrophy and inherited cataract, which are both diseases of the eye leading to premature blindness. There are screening schemes available for these diseases

and all breeding stock should be tested. They should only be bred from if they are within the limits laid down by the scheme's administrators. This is the only way these hereditary diseases are going to be eradicated. Unfortunately, these schemes are only voluntary, but any caring breeder would only breed from stock holding the relevant certificates.

After all the care you have taken so far in finding a suitable puppy, it would be tragic to have your dog becoming prematurely crippled or blinded, sometimes as young as two years old. Therefore, always ask to see the relevant certificates for at least the mother and father of your proposed puppy and even the grandparents if possible. Again, there are no good excuses for the breeder not to have had the dogs tested, and if dogs with a problem in their breed have not been screened for that problem, you need to go elsewhere for your puppy.

The Crossbreed

So far we have discussed only pedigree dogs, but there is a section of the dog population that must not be forgotten. Crossbreeds can have a lot going for them, for one thing, they are not plagued with the hereditary diseases found in so many of their pedigree cousins. Most of them make super pets and companions, but of course their big disadvantage is that it can be a bit of a lottery as to how they are going to turn out. With a pedigree dog, you know pretty well what the adult is going to look like and what his character is likely to be, but with a dog of unknown parentage anything could happen.

If you are going to buy a crossbreed, follow the same guide-lines for buying a pedigree dog. Obviously you will not be involved with a specialist breeder, but make sure you buy direct from the bitch's owner. See the mum and make sure the puppies have been well cared for and socialized. Look for a healthy, well-adjusted individual. I was twelve years old when I had my first dog, a crossbreed of unknown parentage, who went on to become Obedience Champion Lassie's Pride, probably one of the best dogs I have ever owned.

There can be no absolute guarantee that your puppy will be completely flawless in character and free of disease, but by following the guide-lines outlined in this chapter, you are giving yourself the very best chance that in a few weeks' time, the puppy you collect is going to be healthy, of sound mind and character, trainable and a suitable companion for many years to come.

CHAPTER 4

Training Techniques

How a Puppy Learns

In the education process, a puppy is at the same stage as a small child before he has mastered language and reasoning skills. Both learn by experience. If they do something that results in a pleasant experience following, they will repeat that action. On the other hand, if the action results in something unpleasant happening, they will soon learn not to repeat that action. From this, follows one of the basic rules of dog training. When he does something right, praise and reward him. If he does something wrong, scold or punish him.

Up to about twelve weeks of age, a puppy has not yet learnt the difference between what you regard as right or wrong, and what you require of him. You are still establishing your relationship with him and there are two ways of developing his behaviour and training in these early days, avoiding the use of any correction or punishment. The first is by encouraging and praising any action that he does naturally himself, for example, every time he sits, say clearly, 'Sit' and then praise him. Everytime he runs to you, say clearly, 'Come' several times, then praise him and have a game with him when he reaches you. You are teaching him these commands quite effortlessly while he is still a very tiny puppy and without his realizing that training is going on.

The next step is to stop him doing things you do not want him to do. This can be achieved by simply diverting his attention to

something else, thus avoiding a confrontation. At this age, punishment is inappropriate, as he is too young to know what you require. The following example is an excellent illustration of how this diversion method can work. One of the worst problems with young puppies is the chewing of your fingers, a very painful experience as a puppy's milk teeth are like very, very sharp needles. Any waving about of your hands and trying to hit or slap the dog, or jerking your hands away will only attract him further to your hands and excite him more, with what he will now view as a fun game. The easiest way out for you is to distract him with something more enjoyable, start playing with one of his toys. If he is chewing your best furniture or you best shoes, use the same method. Chewing is a common problem with young puppies, but it is something they will grow out of anyway, once their teething problems are over, and it would be a shame to make an issue of it now and ruin your relationship with the puppy. At this stage, you should be aiming to give him as much confidence in you as possible, not constantly chastising and nagging.

Dogs are creatures of habit and learn by constant repetition. Puppies are very forgetful and need to have something shown to them over and over again before they fully grasp it. This needs to be over a period of a few weeks as they only have a very short period of concentration and any training session must not be for more than a few minutes each time.

Rules for Training

- Praise when he responds correctly; scold when he behaves wrongly.

- Praise or punishment must be given at the very instant the action occurs.

- Never give a command unless you are in a position to enforce it.

- Be consistent – dogs learn by habit.

- Never, ever lose your temper.

- Give clear, concise commands.

- Make sure the dog clearly understands what you require.

- Always see things from the dog's point of view.

- Be fair and reasonable in your expectations; do not expect your dog to perform anything he is not capable of.

- Punishment should only be as severe as is needed to stop the action.

- Only punish if you are sure the dog is being disobedient, not just confused.

- Be liberal with your praise.

- Keep training sessions short and enjoyable.

However, once a dog has learnt a lesson thoroughly, he will never forget it. Dogs retired from competition for many years will always remember an exercise when asked to perform it many years after they were last asked. A lesson learnt becomes part of the dog's nature, and it therefore makes sense not to let the puppy learn bad habits which will have to be retrained out later. Prevention is far easier than correction, and it is no harder to teach a dog the right way to behave in the first place, than to teach him the wrong way.

Always try to see things from the dog's point of view. A dog is very often branded disobedient when in fact he is only confused by what you are asking of him. A puppy will only know if his action is right or wrong if he is either praised or scolded at the precise time of the action, not five minutes later. There are many examples of how easy it is to convey the wrong message to your dog when you start training him. How often do you see an owner in the frustrating situation in the park when his dog will just not come back to him. The owner gets crosser and crosser, so much so that when the dog finally does return, he receives a thorough telling off. This might make the owner feel better, but what has the dog learnt? From the dog's point of view coming back to his owner results in punishment: he is unable to reason that he is being told off for his previous actions of running round the park. Is he going to come back so readily next time? It might not seem justice in our eyes, but when the dog did return he should have been praised ecstatically, which would encourage him to return much quicker the next time. However, by the end of this book you will see that the situation should never have been allowed to arise in the first place, and is quite easily avoided.

This same situation can also be used to illustrate another important rule of dog training. Never give a command without being in a position to enforce it. What the dog is learning in the previous example is that if he runs away while you are shouting 'Come' this will motivate you into chasing him around with a lot of excitement, waving arms and raised voices. What a super game for him. The situation will get worse and worse each time he is allowed to indulge in this game. You are reinforcing the behaviour each time it happens and consequently making it more and more difficult to correct. The running away and refusing to return will become a habit that is part of your dog's character.

If, when you go to the park, you know this situation is going to arise, attach a long length of nylon cord to the dog's collar, as well as his lead. In the park remove his lead and let him run free, but still retain hold of the cord. When the command 'Come' is given you are now in a position to reel the dog in to you. Once he is back with you, the fun and praising can start. If this happens every time he is called, the dog will soon associate the command 'Come' with the action of immediately turning round and

Always keep in a position of control. When trying to make a boisterous dog sit, you need control of the head end as well as the rear, otherwise the dog will quite simply run circles round you, in more ways than one! All that is needed here is a shortening of the lead.

running to you. You have put yourself in the position to enforce immediately the command you have given, and avoid any confusion setting in.

This rule is also very relevant to a dog who actually knows the command and starts to defy you. By applying the rule in the situation above, he will soon learn he is unable to gain the upper hand, and so without the use of any harsh punishment or correction, you have again put yourself back in the controlling position.

A dog can only distinguish between a handful of words or commands and, to make it easier for him to learn these quickly, choose commands that are short and sharp to draw his attention to them.

When teaching your dog a new command, do not get involved in a conversation with him. When teaching, for instance, the Sit position, say in a clear, crisp voice his name, followed by 'Sit'. He will not learn the command from a mumble of words thrown at him such as 'Please sit for me and I will give you a biscuit'. When giving a command, give his name first to get his attention (an exception to this being the 'Stay' command). All the family need to be aware of the commands you are going to use, as consistency is another important aid to easy dog training.

Immediately your dog shows any attempt to defy you, put him back on the lead. You are then able to enforce any command you give.

Rewards and Punishments

Your main aid in conveying to your dog whether you are pleased or otherwise is the tone of your voice. Remember, he does not recognize most of the actual words you are saying, but he will understand the intonation in your voice because you are then speaking his language. In his world, a low deep growl from another dog is a threatening warning from a more dominant individual showing displeasure which, if unheeded, usually leads to a physical attack. Only the boldest of dogs ignore it. Use a deep, gruff voice if your dog is being difficult or defiant, thus putting him in the submissive role. A high-pitched yelp expresses pleasure, usually a greeting. It is these tones that your dog is receptive to. He will know when you are pleased with him when you talk to him in a light, high-pitched voice. Reinforce this by physically fussing him when he is good.

Rewards

In addition to using a light, high-pitched tone of voice, and physically fussing your dog, a second, often-used reward, is the giving of titbits. Dogs, in common with all animals, are very food motivated, and this method has always been used by the trainers of performing wild animals, such as dolphins and circus animals. Care must be taken that the dog's attention does not become more centred on the food than on yourself and the lesson you are trying to teach him, but, used in moderation, titbits are certainly an aid in training and can dramatically speed up the process. Bear in mind that their use is more effective on a dog who is hungry and are not very useful after the dog has just had a large meal.

Punishment

Punishment should never need to be given to a puppy under about twelve weeks of age as he will not yet know exactly what is required of him. Before any form of punishment is carried out, it must be clearly established whether he is defying you or whether confusion has set in. For most dogs, it is usually sufficient to administer punishment by the tone of your voice only. If more discipline is required, again look at how dogs act in the wild. A mother disciplines her puppies by getting hold of them by the scruff of the neck and shaking them, an action which carries on to their adult life. A superior dog will grab a subordinate by the neck and shake in the same way. Striking, smacking and hitting dogs with your hands or with newspapers are not generally effective. It is behaviour they do not relate to and they either make a dog fearful and cringing towards you, or, in the case of an excitable dog, the waving about of hands or newspapers will only wind him up more.

Use the dog's eye view again and employ methods he understands: get hold of him by the scruff at the back of his neck, or use two hands either side of his neck, and gently shake him, scolding at the same time and looking him in the eye. This is more than effective for the most difficult dogs.

A shy, nervous dog should never be reprimanded. His training is based on building his confidence, as most of the errors he makes will be caused by his nervousness, and not to outright disobedience. He just does not have the courage or strength of character to do this.

Punishment must always be administered immediately, and should never be prolonged. The short, sharp, instant reprimand is more effective than any of the long-lasting grudges and silences that we humans subject each other to. In any event, after a few minutes, he will have forgotten what he is being cold-shouldered for. Yet again, this kind of action is alien to him, causing him to become more confused about your behaviour. One thing is for sure: he will certainly not be learning to

If punishment is needed, look to how dogs behave in the wild. A mother disciplines her puppies by shaking them by the scruff; a submissive dog always approaches a dominant one with his head down showing his neck, which the dominant dog will grab and shake.

For minor misdemeanours, take the scruff of the neck and gently shake it; for more serious faults, such as aggression, take the dog by the scruff at either side of the neck, lift the front feet off the ground and shake while looking him straight in the eye.

If a young puppy needs to be shown the error of his ways, take him gently by the scruff of the neck and pull him back saying 'No' at the same time.

respect you, the one thing you are trying to cultivate, if you exhibit these human weaknesses to him.

Training Equipment

Collars

The first collar your puppy wears should be a fixed, soft leather collar of a suitable size and strength for him. This type of collar is all that is needed for the first few months, and for a large number of dogs this type of collar will suit them for the rest of their lives.

However, it may be necessary to change to either a half-check collar or a check chain if your puppy is a dominant character who is inclined to pull on the lead. These two collars both work in a similar way and it must be emphasized that a check chain is *not* a choke chain and is not designed to hurt or damage your dog in any way – in fact more harm can be done by a dog constantly pulling hard against a fixed collar – but the theory behind its use needs to be understood in order for you to use it correctly.

A half-check collar or check chain simply enables you to get your dog's attention if you have been unable to obtain it any other way. Hopefully, if you follow the methods outlined further on in this book for getting your puppy to walk on a lead, you should not have a problem with your dog pulling you all over the place in any case.

If any animal has something tight around its neck pulling against it, its reasoning is to pull all the harder to get away from it. Therefore, a

A check chain put on correctly. The large link is able to slide down the chain when the lead is loosened.

dog who has a fixed collar fitting snugly round his neck (which it has to be to avoid the dog slipping out of it) is actually encouraged to pull harder because when he starts to pull against the lead and collar, all you are able to do is pull back against him and the collar will always remain tight round his neck. A vicious circle is started which is then impossible to break, and the situation gets worse.

The principle of the check-chain type of collar is that the chain is always loose round the dog's neck. As the dog starts to pull, the chain tightens putting you back in the same situation as you are with a fixed, tight collar, but the technique is now to very quickly extend your arm. If the collar is fitted correctly, it immediately loosens (the link slides down the chain) and you are then able to give a quick snatch or jerk on the lead. This should not be a powerful, hard jerk, but a short quick movement. The aim is not to hurt the dog physically, but, in the second between the chain going loose and the quick tightening of the chain, to catch the dog's attention and break the circle of both of you pulling against each other. Very often, just the noise of the chain clinking achieves this effect.

The instant you have jerked the lead, you must let the lead go loose again or you will be putting yourself back in the fixed collar, tug-of-war situation, the chain will stay tight round his neck and he will pull against it again. The instant the chain jerks and you get his attention, give a quick command 'Heel', praise him and then try to keep his attention on you.

There is a right and wrong way to put a check chain on your dog. Putting it on the wrong way negates the object of the chain because it cannot release and, consequently, it will get tighter around the dog's neck, which can, of course, be harmful to the dog.

Remembering that the dog is always walked to heel on your left side, the easiest way to practise both the jerking action and putting the chain on the correct way, is to use your left

The incorrect way to use a check chain. The large link is prevented from sliding down and loosening. The collar will get tighter and tighter.

wrist as a substitute for your dog's neck. This will also prove to you how, when used correctly, the chain is harmless and inflicts no pain at all. When put on correctly, the large link of the chain attached to the lead is able to fall and slide down the chain, loosening it around the dog's neck. When put on incorrectly, the large link prevents the chain loosening, and the harder the dog pulls, the tighter the chain becomes, which is totally contrary to what we require.

The half-check collar works on a very similar principle but it is easier to use as there is no right or wrong way of putting it on. The half-check consists of a fixed length of leather or nylon webbing which is joined by a small

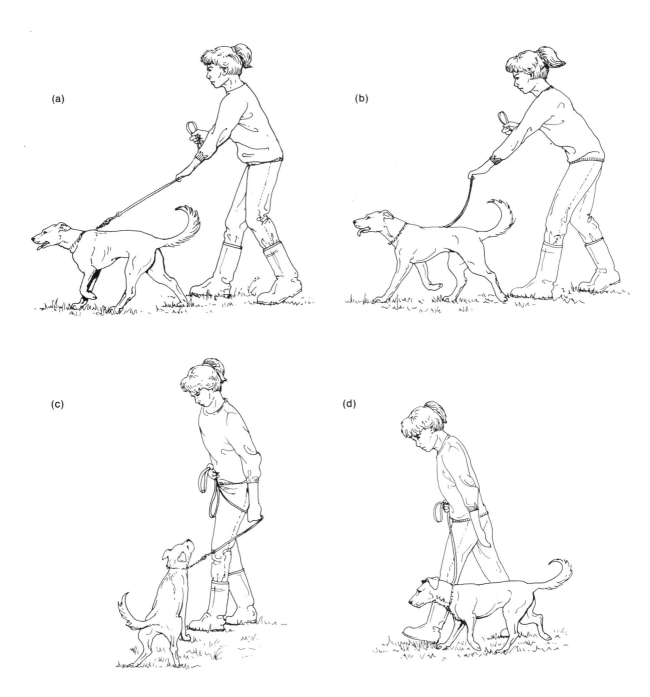

Correct use of the check chain. (a) The dog starts to pull ahead of the handler. (b) As this happens, loosen the lead by extending your arm. (c) Give a quick snatch on the lead. (d) Immediately you let the lead loose, the collar loosens and the dog is at heel. Praise him.

The half-check collar. The D-rings on the collar should just meet, allowing the fixed point of the collar to fit snugly round the dog's neck. This collar is too small and a slightly larger one is now needed.

length of chain. The action is the same as that of a check chain, that is, the collar is relatively loose around the dog's neck and you are able to tighten and release it by a jerking action.

It is important that these chains and collars fit correctly for safety. A correctly fitting check chain should slip over the dog's head easily and, when tightened snugly around the dog's neck, there should be only about 6 inches (15 cm) of spare chain. If it is any longer, so that it dangles down the dog's chest, it is a danger as it is easy for the dog to slip out of it. For a half-check to work effectively, the fixed strapping should meet when fitting snugly tight round the dog's neck. If, when the ends

meet, the collar is still loose round the dog's neck you will not be able to get the action you need, and also your dog could again easily slip out of it.

Choose a collar or check chain suitable to the size and strength of your dog and never buy one of the very, very fine-link check chains as these can cut into the dog. The large, square-link chains are not as effective or free running as the closer linked chains.

Leads

Choosing a lead also requires consideration. Ideally, a lead needs to be about 3 feet (90 cm) long for training purposes, and of a suitable thickness and weight for your dog. A word of advice: if you have a large boisterous dog, a chain lead will hurt and a nylon lead will burn your hands if he does pull on it, so your best bet is a good-quality, supple, leather lead. Make sure also that the hook is of the trigger type as these are safer than the cheaper one-piece hooks, which can be pulled open by a powerful dog.

The Personal Alarm as a Training Aid

The small, pocket-sized personal (or anti-rape) alarms that are now readily available, provide an excellent training aid in several problem situations. The alarm emits a shrill, high-pitched whistle when activated and it is this noise which is effective in helping you to get back in a position of control over your dog.

Its use is discussed in several situations described in this book, but a good example of its effectiveness can be found in the section that deals with the problem of dogs who are noisy while travelling in a car (*see* Chapter 13, page 136).

A dog's hearing is sensitive to higher frequencies than our own, and if all else has failed and you are unable to stop him doing something undesirable by your own voice and actions, the high-pitched shriek is usually enough to stop him in his tracks, giving you the chance to get his attention back on you. Your timing is critical.

The advantage of using the alarm is that he does not necessarily associate the punishment with you and these 'magic' surprise cures are always the ones that work best. The alarms will not harm or hurt a dog's ears, only surprise him or make him uncomfortable. Many vets are actually selling them, but take care when using them near children.

CHAPTER 5

The First Twenty-Four Hours

Planning for your Puppy's Arrival

Now that you have chosen your puppy, you need to arrange with the breeder a time for collecting him. The ideal age to bring a puppy into your home is between seven and eight weeks, as this is a critical developmental stage in his life when he is very receptive. A puppy that is younger than this will not have had the benefit of the interrelationship between his brothers and sisters, and the necessary teachings from his mother. The older he gets, the more independent he becomes and the more difficult it becomes for him to fit in with your family's ways, and for you to establish your role as his leader. Arrange for somebody to be at home full-time for the first week (at

Make sure your house and garden will be safe for your puppy. Trailing electric wires are very inviting for playing with and, of course, chewing, with dire consequences.

least) after you collect him. If a young puppy is left for long periods in a strange place, he will feel abandoned and start to cry, which could well develop into a habit that is hard to break. This week with him is vital as he will gain confidence in both you and his surroundings. If you are really vigilant, it is quite possible for him to be house-trained during the day by the end of the week.

House Rules

Rules need to be established prior to your puppy's arrival home, and all the family need to be involved in these discussions. Everyone must agree on what he is going to be allowed or not allowed to do, and these rules must be adhered to. The puppy will soon become confused and unhappy if one member of the family is encouraging him to do something and another member is telling him off for it. Consistency is one of the main keys to training, and a lack of it will only prolong the training process. Involve any children of the family in these discussions as you will find they will be more helpful in the training if they understand the reasoning behind it. Children will be one of the big influences on your puppy in his early days.

Your basic thinking should be along the lines that you do not let this little bundle of fluff do anything that you will not want a large, muddy adult dog to do. It is far easier to teach a puppy correct habits first than to have to get

Basic manners should be taught from the very beginning. It is as easy to teach good habits as it is to teach bad ones and if each time the puppy jumps up he is pushed down into the Sit, he will learn very quickly that this is the only way he will receive his titbit.

Your puppy should never be allowed to snatch food from you. When he gets older it can be very painful. Early supervision is essential. Praise him when he behaves correctly.

involved in lengthy corrective training procedures to break the established bad habits of an adult dog.

Typical of these family decisions is whether or not your dog is to be allowed on the furniture. Think carefully about it. Carpets will always get a doggy odour on them, but do you really want your armchairs to go the same way? You may not mind the dog hairs that will be on the settee, but will your friends or your business associates be so tolerant of them? You will not be able to explain to your dog that he is only allowed on the furniture when he is dry and that he is banned when he is wet, muddy or in full moult. It is very easy, though, to teach him that he is not allowed on the furniture at all.

The whole family's co-operation is also needed in not giving your puppy titbits at the table. Feeding your dog from the table should not be permitted since he will always pester and beg for food whenever you are eating. It is better to give him any titbits at times when you are not eating yourselves. The full implication of this seemingly simple piece of advice might not be immediately apparent, but cast your mind back to the previous discussions on dominance and leadership. Food and the obtaining of it is still a very powerful force in even a domesticated animal, with direct links

Your puppy's first weeks are the most important of his life with you. He will come to you as a bewildered, confused individual. Let him know he can trust in you, and turn to you for help and comfort. He will more than repay it later.

Let him get used to his own new family (and collar!) before allowing lots of friends in. He may be overwhelmed by too many visitors.

back to his wild ancestor's behaviour. If your dog begs for food and you oblige him, you have immediately put yourself in the sub-ordinate role. You cannot yet tell if your dog is going to be of a dominant nature and confront you with leadership battles, but assume in this case that he is. By giving titbits when he is not expecting them, you are reversing the roles, he is having to accept food on your terms, just as the underdog in the pack would have to. This is also the most difficult rule to make each member of the family stick to!

Decide where the dog is to be allowed free access in the house, will he be allowed upstairs or not. By being consistent with him he can even learn if there are certain areas downstairs to which he is not allowed access.

The First Day

The day you are to collect your puppy, arrange to pick him up early in the morning. This will give him time to settle in with you, and get used to his new surroundings before the trauma of his first night on his own without the comfort of his brothers and sisters. Remember, you are picking up an individual used to the support of his mother. This is your big chance to start building a good relationship

49

with your puppy, as well as establishing your leadership role. In the next few days, he is going to be bewildered and unsure of himself. Everything you do should be aimed at giving the puppy confidence in you, so he will look to you for help, praise and encouragement. There is really no necessity for any punishment or scolding in these few days. He does not yet understand right from wrong, and training should consist only of distracting him from any wrongdoings.

Try to have somebody with you when you collect him from the breeder, so that you can actually hold and look after him in the car. If you have to go on your own, try to obtain a wire travelling cage or a secure box for him to travel in. It will be safer for him than falling about in the car, and he will probably feel more secure.

Although there may be a lot of neighbours and friends who will want to come and visit the new addition, put them off for a couple of days. A lot of strange people and hustle and bustle will only confuse him more. Let him get used to you and your family first.

House-Training

The major thing that has to be sorted out first is the problem of house-training, and this actually starts the moment you arrive home. Puppies will always need to relieve themselves on first waking and after feeding. During the journey home, he will have been confined, so immediately you arrive home take him into the garden and walk round with him, remembering to encourage him all the time, as he will be very unsure of himself. When he does relieve himself, praise and make a fuss of him.

As a responsible dog owner you are going to be teaching your dog to relieve himself on command. It is easily done. Choose a command you feel comfortable with, 'Quickly' or 'Empty' are in common use. If you give this command every time he goes of his own

accord, starting from now, he will soon associate the command with the action, and very soon you will have a dog trained to go on command. The importance of this will become more apparent to you when you start taking your dog out into the local parks and public areas. It is a big help to you and will save a lot of embarrassment if you can make your dog either go before you leave home, or go to a specific area when out so as not to cause offence to anybody. After all, you never see police dogs out on patrol cocking their legs at every shop or lamp post, or fouling the pavements. These dogs started life the same as your puppy did, knowing nothing about social manners, but from day one, their handlers taught them.

The secret of quick house-training is never to let him make a mistake and relieve himself indoors. Each time he does so, the odour (even though you disinfect it) will encourage him to go there again, and the more times he goes indoors, the more the habit will be reinforced. This is why it is so important to arrange to pick up your puppy when somebody will be at home for at least one full week. Every time he wakes up, or immediately after feeding, take him into the garden, walk round with him until he goes, command and praise him. There might be times when he will catch you out, and it is important to have some newspaper on the floor near to the door leading out to the garden. At first, have a large area of paper on the floor and if your puppy starts to puddle indoors, quickly pick him up and put him on the paper to finish off, then praise him. Do not tell him off. The theory behind paper training is that there will be times when you will have to leave him, perhaps to go shopping, and if he is unable to hold himself, he will learn that it is permissible to go on the paper. The paper should be down at all times and he should soon automatically run to it if he does not have access to the garden. If he does persist in puddling on the floors, he needs to be shown that it is wrong. Just point to the misdemeanour and gently scold him, but make sure that this is done immediately. Make sure you praise him each time he uses the paper.

Gradually, over a period of weeks, decrease the area of paper leading towards the door, until eventually there is just one sheet immediately in front of the door. When you then finally dispose of this piece, he should be old enough to be able to hold himself for longer periods, and will wait until he can get into the garden. Every time you do have to leave him, make sure you first take him out in the garden to relieve himself and have a little game with him. He should then sleep while you are out. If, on your return, you let him out straight away, you should have avoided any accident occurring.

House-training is a tedious business, but compare it to potty-training a baby. A puppy learns to be clean in a fraction of the time it takes a baby to learn. It is only a few weeks before he is physically able to hold himself. Unfortunately, there still seems to be some people who think they should 'rub his nose in it' if their dog does go indoors. No one would do that to a baby? What can it possibly achieve if the puppy is too young to hold himself? If you are vigilant and patient a puppy could be clean, or at least paper-trained during the day, within a week.

The First Night

There are now two very different views regarding the best way of getting through the first few nights. The older, more traditional view is that you leave the puppy in his box or basket, usually in the kitchen, covering the floor with newspaper. Of course, the puppy will cry, as he has been left in a dark, strange place without the warmth and comfort of his brothers and sisters. He will be feeling frightened and very lonely, but it has to be said that

if he is left alone, and you ignore his cries, he will quieten down after a few nights. His confidence in his surroundings will be growing each day and he will learn that his cries bring no response from you.

As far as house-training is concerned, he will be going on the newspaper which you will gradually decrease in area, as already described, until eventually you discard it altogether, and he will become clean at nights. This is a far longer process than house-training during the day, first because he is physically unable to hold himself during the night until at least four months of age, and second, the more often he goes on the paper the more it becomes the acceptable thing to do.

Now consider another method which has been used very successfully in more recent times. Puppies trained this way usually become clean much quicker and are generally much more reliable with very few mishaps.

This method involves taking him from night one into your bedroom. This is not to say that he will be spending his nights with you forever more, because once he regards your home as his own, it is a relatively easy process to move his bed downstairs. Even if he cries for one night when you do this, he will soon stop if you do not go to him. He is not crying from fear, but only because he is a bit put out about the change of routine. There are, however, two very big advantages in using this method. First, you are yet again building on your relationship with the puppy: if he is in his box beside your bed and starts whimpering, you can just put a hand out to him and comfort him, and once again he will have looked to you for help and confidence. Second, puppies always wake at first light and will immediately relieve themselves. You will have surrounded his box or bed with newspaper and you will hear it rustle as he starts to move around. It means your getting up straight away and taking him down to the garden, but you will again have been successful in avoiding a puddle in the house, and the less he goes in the house, the less you are reinforcing the acceptability of it, and the easier it is eventually to get him clean.

House Training without a Garden

This can present some difficulties and the easiest way to start house-training in this situation is to paper-train the puppy exactly as previously explained. Just as with training in the garden, walk him around on the paper until he goes, giving him the appropriate command, and then praise him. At first you will need a large area of paper but gradually this can be decreased until he is confined to a small area. With the small toy breeds, it is then possible to use a large cat-litter tray lined with newspaper, and it is possible for this method to be used permanently. With a larger breed, however, once they are old enough to hold themselves for longer periods, you need to dispose of the paper and start taking him out. Without the convenience of a garden, it is more important to establish a regular routine so that the dog will get to know the times he is going to be taken out to relieve himself. Make sure that the interval between each trip is not longer than four hours.

Establishing a Feeding Routine

There are two important lessons that can be easily taught at mealtimes: one is the introduction of the 'Sit' command, and the other is that he is not to be possessive or aggressive over his food and possessions. Your puppy will start by having three or four meals per day, and in the first few days you may have to coax and encourage him to eat. However, once he is eating readily the training procedure should be introduced straight away.

It does not take much forethought to see that an adult dog who is aggressive over his food is a threat to family peace and harmony. A dog who is possessive over his food is also more likely to be possessive over his toys and possessions. The consequences of this are that you will have to be on guard virtually twenty-four hours a day to make sure that nobody, children or visitors, approach your dog at mealtimes or when he is lying near his toys. Obviously, this is a totally unacceptable situation, and aggression in any form is something which must not be allowed to develop in even the tiniest of puppies. Yet again, it is easier not to let the habit develop in the first place than to cure it in an adult dog.

When your puppy has been given his dinner, just occasionally take the bowl away from him. Praise him as you take it, and then immediately give it back to him. Do not do it too often or you will make him edgy and worried; just once at each feedtime is sufficient. Any aggression shown should be immediately checked by getting the scruff of the neck and scolding him. Be as firm as is needed to stop the show of aggression – it has to be stopped. When you give the food back, praise him. There are not many puppies who will be aggressive at this age and most are just too interested in looking for the food. The lessons you are teaching him, though, are vital. Also practise this exercise with any bone or toy he may be playing with. Any person in the house should be able to do this, even the smallest child, as they are the ones who will be most at risk if the dog does grow up to be possessive. This exercise must not be allowed to develop into an excuse for any children to tease him, and they must be carefully supervised.

Mealtimes are also ideal for introducing the 'Sit' command. Your aim is to have a dog who, when waiting for his dinner, sits patiently until you put his dish down and tell him he can have it. You are trying to avoid your dog getting over-excited at mealtimes, jumping up and

Start the right routine when your puppy is young and you will have no problem when he is grown up. He should wait until you tell him to have his dinner. The alternative is the chaos of an undisciplined dog jumping up and knocking everything out of your hands.

knocking the dish out of your hand as you put it down. Again, teach the correct habits early. Each time you feed him, put him into the Sit position, making sure you give the command clearly. As explained in the next chapter, at first he will probably just get up, but be persistent and he will soon learn that he has to conform to get his dinner, and believe me it will not take him long to learn!

CHAPTER 6

The Early Weeks

House Manners

There is an old saying that you cannot start training a dog until he is six months old. Do not believe it. It may apply to the strictly formal training required for the top-class competitive exercises, but basic training must start from the day a puppy is taken away from his mother and enters his new home. If a dog is allowed to run riot and is offered no guide-lines to the behaviour expected of him, by the time he is six months old he will be a delinquent adolescent used to having his own way. He may also be a strong, boisterous adolescent and you may not have the physical strength that would, by then, be required to keep him in control and bring him to order. His manners, attitudes and character are being formed from the time he is born, and the period up to about sixteen weeks of age is the most formative in his life. It is at this age that any potentially nervous or aggressive problems can be identified and dealt with easily, so that such puppies then have the chance to develop into well-adjusted, much-loved and wanted adults.

Having already established the rules of your house, you now have to start applying them. You might be met with resistance, but provided your rules are fair and reasonable in the first place, do not give way. Just as children do, he is learning how far he can push you and if you relent at the first hurdle, your authority will always be undermined.

The first difference of opinion is often met when he decides the furniture looks more comfortable than his own bed or the floor. As he tries to climb up, push him back saying 'No' firmly. Shows of temper will often be displayed by a bossy puppy and this may be apparent in his biting and chewing your hands. If he gets his way now he will learn that shows of defiance (and even aggression) will get the result he wants. Obviously, this will create serious problems when he reaches adulthood. Any acts of defiance must be stopped, and usually, just a firm voice and determined attitude is all that is needed from you at this stage. It is equally important, that you give plenty of praise and reward when he does well. If you are successful in these early confrontations, he will not challenge you later.

Leaving your Puppy Alone

Something your puppy has to get used to is being left on his own and it is important that this is done correctly from the beginning. If the puppy is suddenly left for very long periods of time, he is likely to become bored, destructive and very often noisy, and once these habits are allowed to develop they are extremely difficult to cure.

The best way to accustom him to the situation is to leave him for only a short period of time at first: go into another room for a short while and listen for his reactions. Start establishing the routine you will use when you have

Having told your puppy he is to get off the chair, you must make him. He must not be allowed to defy you and win.

If any resistance is met when pushing him back, it must be stopped now. If he learns he can get his own way now, you will not stand a chance of controlling him when he is fully grown.

to leave him for longer periods: take him into the garden to relieve himself, and have a game with him so that when you leave him he will be tired and more than likely ready to go to sleep. However, in case he is not, leave him with plenty of his own toys to play with (removing your own best shoes or slippers from harm's way). Make sure you leave temptation out of reach. If food is left out which is easy to reach he will help himself to it, and will then always be on the lookout for it when he is left, raiding bins and cupboards. If he never has the opportunity to thieve, the habit will not develop.

Before leaving him, remember to put newspaper on the floor. Tell him to 'Wait' and leave him in the room. Avoid hesitating or sympathizing with him and leave confidently. He will probably whimper and cry, but do not go running straight back to him. After a short while he will stop, either to sleep or to investigate his toys. When he does go quiet, return to him and praise him. Only return during a quiet period. Gradually build up the time you leave him, and he will soon become confident that he has not been abandoned and that you will always return.

Destructive Behaviour

Puppies who are left alone are usually destructive for two reasons: boredom and teeth-

55

Puppies are constantly looking for things to chew. If left on their own indoors without any toys they could well start on your furniture. Always make sure that your puppy is not chewing anything that could be harmful. This small stick was removed from the puppy as it could have got stuck in his throat.

There are several methods for stopping your puppy chewing your fingers. Do not wave your hands about to excite him more. Take him by the scruff of the neck and pull him back saying 'No'.

ing problems. Playing with him before he is left helps relieve the first as he is likely to go straight to sleep. Leaving a juicy marrow bone or one of the large dog chews can help save your furniture. Puppies have to chew before they get their adult teeth, but unfortunately, some seem to have more of a problem than others. If he does start on the fittings and furniture, there are special foul-tasting sprays available, which you can apply to the items at risk. They do not harm the furniture, and can be very effective provided they are used as soon as the problem starts, and that there are alternatives to hand for the puppy to chew on.

These sprays are available now from most pet stores.

Teething can be a painful experience for you as well as for your puppy. Your hands, ankles and feet are very attractive moving objects to him, but his milk teeth, which are like sharp needles, can cause problems, especially when children are about.

The more you wave and flap your hands about, the more excited your puppy will become, so keep calm and move slowly. Distract his attention from you by playing with his toys. If that is ineffective, then you need to let him know this behaviour is unacceptable. Move one hand round to the back of his neck and pull him back by the scruff saying firmly

'No'. Be only as firm as is needed to make him stop, no more. Alternatively, you could push your hand into his mouth, which is most uncomfortable for him and he will soon realize that this is not such a fun game after all.

Socializing

You cannot take your puppy out for walks or to meet other dogs before he has finished his course of vaccinations, usually by about fourteen weeks of age. However, this is an important time in his life for character forming and socializing, and for identifying and remedying any personality faults he may have.

Give your puppy a few days to get used to you and his new surroundings and then start gradually introducing him to as many people as you can, men, women and children. If he appears to be apprehensive, keep the situation well controlled.

Avoid letting too many visitors in at once, which will only overwhelm him. Let him take everything one step at a time. Ask your visitor to kneel down to his level, as this is not so threatening as somebody towering above and reaching down to him, and ask him to encourage the puppy gently but not force himself on him. As his confidence gradually increases, he will be able to cope with the hustle and bustle of more people, but take it slowly.

If your puppy shows any aggression to any visitor, this must be stopped *now*. Identify whether the agression is caused by fear. If it is, his confidence needs to be built up as outlined above. If it is not, then he needs to know this behaviour is totally unacceptable. Take him by the scruff, shake and scold him. Be as firm as is needed to stop the action. When he stops, the visitor should then stroke and praise him. Even if you have no children yourself, any dog should learn to accept them and their ways, so 'borrow' some from your friends. Most puppies love playing with children provided the games are well supervised, and the children are not allowed to tease or win all the time.

Although he cannot be taken out for walks yet, he needs to be taken into the wide world to get used to traffic noises, large lorries, crowds and so on. At this age, the secret is to introduce him gradually to different and, in his eyes, frightening situations until he accepts them as normal. This is especially important with a puppy of a slightly nervous disposition.

If he is confronted with these situations in his formative weeks, he will cope with them quite easily. It is too late to leave this until his vaccinations are completed. This is also a chance to get him used to the car. Just take a short journey, say to the shops, and then carry him from the car. At first, choose a time when you know it will be reasonably quiet and, gradually, over a period of a couple of weeks introduce him to busier crowds and traffic. A good place to take him, if possible, is to the local primary school at turning-out time. Most young puppies have no trouble accepting these new things and take them in their stride, but if he is worried, do not sympathize with him because this will make it appear that he does have a real reason to worry. Talk to him and stroke him as if everything is normal. If he feels that you are confident, his worries will soon go.

Greeting Visitors

There are three attitudes your puppy could adopt towards visitors coming to your home, and each will need training in different ways. First, he could be nervous of them, which means that he will need gradual, careful introductions to different people, as explained above. Second, he could be too aggressive towards them which *must* be stopped now. Third, he could get too excited and make a nuisance of himself. It is for this last reason that the 'bed routine' can be so helpful. Your puppy will already have his own area or bed where he sleeps, and the easiest routine to adopt is to make him go to his bed until everyone is in and settled. You can then call him for a fuss or greeting at your leisure. You are achieving two things this way: first, you are making it easy for everyone to get in and settled without the dog becoming over-excited and getting in everyone's way; second, you are reinforcing your position as the leader. To teach him to go to bed on command is easy. Every time he goes to his bed of his own accord, just say the command 'Bed' in a clear voice, and praise him. He will soon learn the command. When he is familiar with the command, you can then teach him to go to bed as and when you want him to. Give the command 'Bed', take him to his area and make him lie down. Praise him.

When you do call him to greet everybody, ask your visitors to bend down, or at least be sitting down to greet your puppy, that is, come down to his level. This is not so intimidating for a nervous puppy, or as a threatening to an aggressive one. It also helps to stop the puppy learning to jump up, but if he does, push him down saying 'No' firmly. Everybody needs to be consistent on this, and if one visitor keeps insisting that it does not matter, you will have to be as firm with that person as you are with your puppy, who will never learn not to jump up if some people encourage him to do so. Explain to them that you need their help as you are training your puppy not to jump up at people. After all, if he was fully grown and just been out for a muddy walk, they would not like him climbing all over them. Most people will co-operate when you explain it to them in this way.

Barking and excessive noise is another thing that can become a problem when people arrive. There is nothing wrong with him barking when somebody knocks at the door. However, incessant barking is not desirable as your dog will then be the cause of many complaints from your neighbours. The easiest way to control the problem is to teach him to speak on command, and then stop when told, that is, teach barking as a proper exercise. When he barks, whether it be when someone calls or for any other reason, tell him to 'Speak' and then praise him. Then command him, in a deep, stern voice 'Stop' or 'Enough' or whatever the command is that you choose. Insist that he stops, and again, at this young age, distracting him with something else is the easiest way; then start to play with him. If this is done every time he starts to bark, he will soon learn both commands, which will put you back in a position of control.

Guarding

This is an area of your dog's development that requires serious consideration because of the consequences that can arise if the training goes wrong. If you have taught and encouraged your puppy to guard his property, do not be fooled into thinking that you will be able to control him when he is an adult. Even if you think you would have the physical strength to do so, you will also have to outwit him as well, and his fighting instincts and reflexes are far more developed than yours ever will be. If he has been taught to guard, there will come a time when he will challenge you for full leadership. When this confrontation occurs and his teeth are used with meaning, your own physical power counts for very little.

Even before this confrontation does occur, if your dog has been taught to guard and be aggressive, *you* are in fact the one who will have to be on guard twenty-four hours a day. An innocent child might wander in when you have accidentally left the dog out, or play-fighting games between members of your family can be misinterpreted by such a dog, with dire consequences. This may sound over-dramatic, but it is happening more and more frequently and making so many headlines. Unfortunately, certain breeds are then maligned as 'dangerous breeds', to be banned or specially licensed. The only reason these dogs are dangerous in any way, is that they attract the wrong people to own them, people who just want a 'walking burglar alarm' or want to improve their 'macho' image.

Looking at your small innocent puppy now, you may not be able to believe that the above could possibly apply, but time after time at pet classes, owners will come for a few weeks with one of the guarding breeds. If these dogs show any aggressive tendencies, such owners are told how to stop them and the reasons why, but instead of heeding the advice, they invariably leave disgruntled, their reasoning being that 'I bought this dog because I want him to protect me and attack burglars'. So often, these people return months later wanting either information on how to rehome the dog, as he has now bitten their children, neighbours, and so on, or wanting help to train the dog, as he only defies them. Unfortunately, the situation by then is so hopelessly out of control that the dog invariably ends up being discarded or destroyed. As puppies there was nothing wrong with these dogs. In the right hands, they could have grown up into super, impressive dogs, whose mere presence in the house is enough to deter any burglar in any case. Even a small dog is going to bark and alert everybody. There is nothing wrong with appreciating a dog's value as a deterrent to would-be burglars, but this should not be a principal reason for obtaining him.

Collar and Lead Training

A young puppy should wear only a soft leather collar suitable for his size, never a check chain of any sort. His collar can be put on in the first few days (remember to add a small name and address tag). He will probably not like it and will shake and try to scratch it off. Do not sympathize with him, but distract his attention to something more interesting.

Getting him used to walking on a lead should always be done indoors or in the garden, and not left until the first time he goes out for a walk in the outside world. He will have enough to worry about that day, without being dragged along on a lead.

Only put a lead on him when he is completely used to wearing his collar. Choose a lightweight lead and avoid drawing too much attention to it when you attach it. Start to walk off, encouraging him to run after you. Try not to let the lead go taut, dragging him along. This will only worry him and make him pull against it to get away. If he really seems worried, try titbits to entice him to follow you, or let go of the lead so that he gets used to it being attached without being restricted on it. If he starts to pull on the lead, do not start to do anything physically to stop him, such as jerking him back to you. It needs correcting, but an easy way to stop him pulling is for you to keep changing direction. Each time he pulls ahead of you, turn round and start to walk the other way. Encourage him to bounce along by your side by holding a plaything. This is all that is needed at this early stage.

When he is quite unconcerned about having the lead put on, start the correct routine you will use when he is older. Put him in the Sit position while putting on the lead. Before taking it off, make him sit and stay there while you remove it. Praise and release him.

Introducing the Basic Commands

'Sit' and 'Stay'

Teach your puppy the 'Sit' command very early in his education. It is very easy to teach and it is also an extremely useful exercise for your dog to know.

Accustom your puppy to walking on the lead before he actually has to go out in the wide world. If he is reluctant, do not drag him along, but gently encourage him to move by enticing him with his toy or a titbit.

Introduce the command by saying 'Sit' every time your puppy sits of his own accord, and he will soon associate the action with the command. To make him sit at your request, push his hindquarters down at the same time as giving the command clearly. Be careful not to push in the middle of his back, but right down near the base of his tail. You may need to support his front end or hold on to his collar to prevent his turning round or running off. Try not to let him jump up immediately but keep him in the 'Sit' position for a few seconds before releasing and praising him.

Once he appears to understand 'Sit' and is happy complying with it, you can introduce the 'Stay' command. Gradually increase the time you keep him in the Sit, saying 'Stay' clearly all the time. Avoid using his name as this will encourage him to get up, and always be ready to put your hand on his hindquarters the instant he looks as if he is going to move. It is easier if you kneel down beside him when first teaching the exercise as he is less likely to get up if you are not standing above him, and you are also more likely to be able to catch him if he moves. Release and praise him only when he is staying quite steadily and without restraint. Never get exasperated, give up and let him win; you must persevere until he stays if only for a few seconds. Be patient and never lose your temper with him if he keeps getting up; for it is you who are not anticipating his actions fast enough, and he cannot be expected to know immediately what you require.

Introducing the 'Sit' command. Push the dog's hindquarters down, while supporting his front end. Note that the handler is pushing right at the base of the tail, not in the middle of his back, which could hurt him.

Always make him Sit before giving him his dinner.

Once he knows the 'Sit' command, always make him sit for his dinner and for having his lead put on. If you start this from the very beginning you will soon find he will automatically go into the Sit at these times without any command from you, a far happier situation than the alternative chaos of an untrained dog being shouted at, knocking everything over and upsetting everybody.

'Recall'

Another exercise that is so very easily introduced during a puppy's very early weeks is the Recall. He is going to be doing this exercise many times a day of his own accord, in fact, every time he runs to you. All you have to do is to start associating in his mind the command 'Come' with the action.

Each time your puppy runs after you or comes towards you, say clearly, 'Come', then praise and fuss him when he reaches you. Make sure he hears the command clearly and that you do not jumble it up with a lot of other chatter. He has to hear that command plus his name clearly and to see that you are happy when he is running towards you. Open your arms as a visual signal to him.

When he has been with you a few days and has settled in, enlist the help of another member of the family and set up fun situations. Run away while someone restrains him for a few seconds and then releases him to

Introducing the Recall. Each time the puppy runs to you, give the command 'Come' and let him see you are pleased to welcome him. With this very young puppy, the handler is kneeling down to his level so as not to encourage jumping up, or to appear intimidating.

Always praise your puppy when he comes to you and occasionally give him a titbit. He has to know it is always fun to come to you.

chase after you. When preparing his dinner, let someone hold him the other side of the room and, when his dinner is ready, let him go. Every time, you must make sure he hears the command 'Come' quite clearly and that you really fuss him when he reaches you. At this young age, there should be nothing done that is too formal; just keep it fun.

Preparing for Visits to the Vet and the Groomer

The Vet

At various times during your dog's life, he is going to have to visit the vet. This can either be a pleasurable experience for him, or it can be intolerable. It depends very much upon you which way it will go. Your vet is at a very great disadvantage when he tries to treat your dog. Your dog cannot tell him what is wrong or how he is feeling. Armed only with the information you can give him such as 'he is off colour and not himself', your vet has to try to ascertain the problem. This involves a lot of feeling, touching and observing the dog's reaction. If your dog is struggling so hard and being totally uncooperative, this job is made almost impossible and very often remedies have to be tried and tested based on the little information the vet can glean from you. Your dog's course of treatment could, therefore, take longer and

Lift the skin around his mouth to examine his teeth regularly. This picture clearly shows the sharp needle-like milk teeth.

cost more than if the problem is immediately identified.

Your puppy needs to learn to be a model patient from a young age, and it only takes a few seconds a day to accustom him to being examined. This time does not have to be specially put aside; it can be incorporated into the time you spend playing with your puppy. He needs to get used to you touching his feet, his mouth and his ears, and to stand still while you run your hands over him. His feet are usually the most sensitive, so while you are fussing him, handle his feet and nails and try to examine between the toes and the pads underneath the foot. Hold on to his foot quite firmly and if he pulls away do not let his foot go. As he draws his foot away from you, hold on to it firmly but go with it. Praise him all the

This young puppy is already quite unperturbed about having his ears examined. He will be an easy patient for his vet in years to come.

Some dogs need regular, thorough grooming. It is so much easier and pleasurable if, from puppyhood, the dog has been trained to accept the procedure. This long-haired German Shepherd Dog positively enjoys it.

time and persevere. Once he has learnt that you are not going to let go and that you are not going to hurt him, you will be able to examine his feet without any struggling on his part.

Get him used to his mouth being handled and examined by gently lifting the skin around his mouth, then examining his teeth. Ears often need veterinary attention because they can get dirty and, in the summer, grass seeds can get lodged down inside the ear. If your dog will let the vet look down the ears without any resentment, it will save him the indignity (and further expense) of being muzzled, manhandled, tranquillized or even anaesthetized. His first visit to the vet will be when he is about ten weeks old and if you have already accustomed him to this handling before this visit, the experience will not be so traumatic and will reduce the likelihood of any worry on his future visits. Most vets go out of their way to make your puppy's first visit a happy occasion.

It is not in his interest to have an unco-operative patient, but he needs your help in achieving this.

The Groomer

If you have a breed that is going to require specialized grooming and clipping, you must introduce him to the routines as early as possible. Most poodle breeders will already have given their puppies a light clipping on their face and feet before they leave for their new homes. This gets them used to the noise and feel of the clippers and of being handled.

Even if your dog will not require clipping and trimming, he needs to learn to accept grooming as a regular part of his life and you need to start as early as possible, even if he does not need full grooming yet. Be patient with him and make the grooming sessions short and enjoyable.

CHAPTER 7

First Outings

When your puppy has finished his course of inoculations, he will be able to go for walks in the outside world. At this stage, he should already be well on the way to becoming a well-mannered, well-adjusted individual, looking to you for guidance and leadership. He will be happy, contented, will know exactly where he stands, which means that a major part of your training has already been achieved because once his attitude is right, the rest of the training is relatively simple, provided you carry on with the principles you have learnt. Bear in mind, that as he approaches adolescence, he may try to get the upper hand, but any challenges should now be nipped in the bud quickly and easily.

Road Safety

Your dog, along with any other member of society, has to learn to be safe on the roads and be aware of other road users. Obviously you cannot teach him the Green Cross Code, as we would our young children; we have to approach the problem in a different way. The aim is to make sure that your dog does not cause any accidents by either running into the path of oncoming traffic or by distracting drivers. The dog cannot think logically that if he runs in the road, the chances are that a car could hit him, or swerve to miss him, causing a more serious accident.

We can, however, quite easily teach him

A dog dashing straight into the road can cause a driver to swerve, thinking the dog will carry on running. He may not see the lead attached or he may think the handler has lost control anyway.

that every time he approaches a kerb, he must sit automatically and only go forward when given the command to do so. The training starts the first time you go out with your puppy along the streets. Your puppy will already

A dog's kerb drill. At every kerb, stop. Do not let the dog step into the road.

Shorten the dog's lead and put him into the Sit.

know how to sit on command, so every time you approach a kerb, put him into the Sit position. Make him stay there until you are ready to move off, then give him the command 'Heel' and encourage him to come with you. As always, consistency is the key, and you must do this at every kerb you come to during your walks. In a very short time, he will automatically sit every time he reaches a road and you will eventually reach the stage when he will not cross a road until he has sat first.

It must be emphasized that even when this degree of reliability has been achieved, your dog should never be off the lead when walking along the street. There is always the unexpected that you cannot prepare for, such as another dog attacking him or chasing what it thinks is an unaccompanied dog, or a car backfiring close to the dog, frightening him and causing him to bolt into the path of another car. It is also very distracting for

When he has sat, praise him. Only let him get up as you set off across the road, giving the command 'Heel'.

drivers seeing a loose dog running up to a road. Although you may know that your dog will stop at the kerb, the driver does not and he could swerve or brake hard and cause an accident to occur.

Walking to Heel

The ideal position you want your dog to adopt when walking with you is just slightly ahead of you, near to your left leg, with the lead loose. When you meet people you want to speak to, your dog should sit beside you and wait until you are finished and ready to continue. He should not jump up at them or continually be pulling you to get at other dogs or people who may be passing. This type of heelwork is not to be confused with the competitive style you see in the obedience competitions; in fact, if you tried to teach your dog such precision at this stage, you would only spoil him if you wanted to compete at a later date. The competitive heelwork is taught as a completely different exercise altogether, with a different set of requirements and commands, and is described fully later on.

When you first take your puppy out for a walk along the streets, he is unlikely to pull you because he will be very unsure of himself and you will probably need to encourage him to walk with you. If he does hang back, do not pull or drag him along, worrying him all the more. It is always upsetting to see young children dragging tiny puppies along the road who are obviously on their first outings. A puppy with a slightly nervous disposition could have his character ruined for life by bad experiences such as this, so early in his education. Encourage him all the time, bend down to him and coax him along. Wait for him if he wants to rest or to take stock of his surroundings, but do not sympathize with him. When your puppy has gained in confidence and perhaps does start to pull, there is an easy

Not a very relaxing or enjoyable way to go for a walk. The owner needs to move his right shoulder forward so that the lead goes loose for a second. At that instant he needs to give a quick sharp jerk on the lead to get the dog's attention. To get back in a position of control, put the dog in the Sit and start again. The lead should be jerked before the situation occurs again.

method to stop him, which works well if started early enough. As he starts to go ahead of you, change direction, turn about and walk away from him. As he looks to you and chases after you, praise him and generally try to get his attention on you, and what you are doing. A dog that is always conscious of his owner's actions is not going to be a 'puller'.

As you can appreciate, these early training sessions are outings on their own with no other purpose than to get him used to walking with you. Your puppy should not be out for

Pippa showing her two styles of heelwork. She is not expected to perform her competitive style while out walking along the streets.

long walks in any case; and you will not be able to spend the necessary time and care doing the above training if you are rushing up to the shops, or to collect the children, or whatever.

If you have a dominant type of puppy, the above method may not be completely successful and you will need to do more formal training using a half-check collar or check chain, but you need only change over to one of these when it becomes apparent that the pulling is going to be a real problem. You do not want the problem to become established and, therefore, more difficult to correct, but you need to determine when it is necessary to start using a half-check. It will depend a lot on your own puppy, but in most cases it should

not need to be used before six months of age. (If you are having a problem with a puller, it is also an early indication that he is attempting to take over leadership and you need to look carefully at your attitudes towards your dog indoors.)

Before starting the treatment for this problem, you should have already mastered the technique of correctly using a half-check chain (*see* page 41). The easiest way to start each training session is to put the dog in the Sit at your left-hand side. You are then putting yourself in the position of control to start with. The lead is already loose and, as you start to walk off, say clearly to the dog 'Heel' in a stern voice. As he rushes off, do not let the lead

These two lads and their well-trained dogs can actually enjoy their outings together.

tighten, but quickly give him a short sharp jerk at the same time saying 'Heel'. The jerk will distract him long enough for you to praise him and get his attention. If he rushes off again, repeat the process. The lead must be loose at all times, except for the instant of the jerk. Eventually he will try less and less to rush off, and will stay close to you. Make sure you continually praise him when he is with you, and even give him titbits to get his attention. If you think you are losing control of the situation, always go back to the Sit position, that is, put yourself back in control and start again.

Once you have started this training, it is vital to be consistent. A week's training can be ruined if one day you decide you cannot be bothered, and let him drag you everywhere. It may seem a tedious few weeks, but remember, once he knows he cannot pull you everywhere, he will be a pleasure to take out for the rest of his life.

A couple of tips to help you with a very difficult dog: first, do not take him on a regular route, say to the park, if you are still struggling with the heelwork problem. If he knows he is going somewhere he enjoys, he will be more single-minded in pulling to get there, and more likely to throw caution to the wind. You really are then fighting an uphill battle. Second, be one step ahead of him in anticipating his actions. If you know he is always going to pull towards another dog, make sure you see any dogs first and be ready for your dog's reaction. Do not allow yourself to be pulled off your feet first. Maintain your position of authority and if a situation is threatening, jerk him just fractionally before he makes off. Timing is critical in dog training, and never more so than in this situation.

As far as meeting people in the street is concerned, there should not be a problem with your puppy jumping up, as this is something you will already have been working on with him since he arrived in your home. You now just need to establish the routine you wish him to adopt when you are out, and the best

Your dog should not be allowed to jump up at people he meets in the street, whether they are strangers or friends. You could soon become very unpopular.

As you approach someone, shorten the lead ready to put your dog in the Sit.

With your dog in the Sit, you can now relax knowing that he will not embarrass you nor annoy your friend.

way is for him to automatically go into the Sit when you stop walking. Again, you have already been teaching him to do this by sitting him at every kerb you approach. You may be pleasantly surprised, he may already have learnt to sit of his own accord every time you stop. If he does not, each time you meet somebody just put him into the Sit as normal and tell him to 'Stay' just as you have already been doing indoors. Everybody is then happy, your friend can fuss the dog or talk to you, you are proud of your dog, and the dog is happy as he is not getting shouted at.

Meeting Other Dogs

Early experiences are very important so you should try to make sure your puppy only meets well-behaved, non-aggressive dogs during his early months. For most puppies, their first encounters with strange dogs provide no

A far happier situation for the dog as well. He can now have a fuss without any of the shouting and general chaos. Dogs are happy when they know what is required of them.

When approaching other dogs on the lead, your dog should be at Heel and under control.

You will then be able to maintain control as you pass the other dog.

problems or difficulties whatsoever. Having been taken from their own mother at the right age (i.e. not before seven weeks) they will have been well taught and sufficiently socialized with dogs to know exactly how to react and cope with others of their own kind. However, some puppies find it a little more difficult and require some help. They could either react nervously or aggressively, although usually, aggression is only a sympton of the fear that the puppy may feel as a result of his being unsure of himself. Provided you are certain of the temperament, and know the other dog, you need to portray to your puppy an air of confidence, showing him that there really is nothing to fear. If you sympathize with him too much, he will conclude that there really is something to worry about. Try to encourage him to meet the other dog, and stroke him yourself. If he really is worried, carry on

If your dog is already out of control as you approach another dog, you will have no chance of being in command if the dogs take a dislike to each other.

walking with him, distracting him from his worry about the other dog.

Do not at this stage force a face-to-face confrontation. Leave it for a few weeks, carrying on as above and you will find his confidence will gradually come. If it appears that any aggression is really meant then this must be stopped immediately by the methods you are now familiar with. He has to know it will not be tolerated and that he has no right to start a fight with someone else's dog. In any case, one day he will meet more than his match and will be the one to come off second best. Once he is used to, and comfortable with other dogs, obviously you want him to enjoy himself and play with them, but always make sure he will come back when you call him.

The Recall

This subject has already been touched upon in Chapter 4 as an illustration of how easy it is for us to fail to get our message across to our dog. We shall now take this exercise step by step from the beginning, in order to obtain a reliable, instant recall from our dog at all times.

Your puppy will already have an idea of the command 'Come' as you will already have been using the command each time he has run to you indoors. We now have to extend this so that he will come to us on command, at our whim each and every time, and not just when he feels like it.

If utilized properly, the first couple of days that you take him to the park can give you a very sound basis for a reliable Recall. Try to find a park that is well enclosed or fenced on all sides, with perhaps just an opening for the car park, or somewhere that is safe and well away from the roads. Make sure that there are no unknown dogs about (that is, dogs that could frighten or even attack your puppy) and then take his lead off, having already attached

a long length of very fine nylon cord to his collar as a precaution. On his first time out, there is no way your puppy is going to take off and run away from you. He will do quite the opposite. He will be unsure of himself and will either stand still or run towards you. So make the most of this and run away from him, not too far, and encourage him to chase after you. Make a game of this so that your puppy learns this is fun and worth his while to come to you. All the time he is running after you make sure he is hearing the command 'Come' clearly.

When he reaches you, make a fuss of him. Just do several short bursts of this. It is important not to overtire a young puppy. You will only have the advantage of this receptive time for a couple of days, because after that he will gain confidence and be more prepared to go off and do his own thing and investigate. But with a lot of dogs, this early training is all that is needed to have a reliable dog who will instantly turn round and run towards you every time you call him. He will find the 'game' you have taught him is better than anything he can do himself. You could, of course, reinforce his pleasure at coming to you by giving titbits as he reaches you.

If, after a few weeks (or maybe only days with a dominant dog), you find he is not responding instantly every time you call him, then more formal training is required immediately. He should only ignore you once for you to take more positive action. If he ignores your command and he is off the lead, he will quickly realize that you are in no position to enforce it. If this happens, *never* make the fatal mistake of chasing after him because you will teach him that if he ignores you, a great game of chasing will follow. The first time he ignores you, there is not a lot you can do about it that particular day. You will have to be patient and wait until he returns to you. Hold on to your temper, do not hit him or shout at him when he returns. You do not want to frighten him off ever wanting to come back

Always make your dog sit in front when he comes to you in order to give you more control and time to put his lead back on before he decides to run off again.

to you. If you really feel you cannot say anything nice (and who can blame you) then do not say anything at all. Go home. However, the next day, go out prepared.

Take with you a very, very long length of fine nylon cord. Attach this to his collar just prior to taking his lead off, and then make a fuss of actually removing the lead. Let the nylon line trail so that he feels he is actually free. When you are ready, call him. If he ignores you, immediately jerk the line, no matter how far away he is, and start reeling him in to you. This will initially come as a great shock to him, and he will not usually defy you again. You have again achieved success by keeping to one of the rules of dog training: *never give a command unless you are in a position to enforce it.* When you have reeled him in, do not forget the praise and the titbits if used.

With a dog that persistently runs off, you will need to keep this cord handy at all times so that he never has the chance to ignore you. Only when he is consistently turning and returning instantly on your command, can you dispense with it. Never be afraid to go back to its use if need be; you will find that dog training often proceeds by two steps forward, one step back in order to reinforce a particular point.

When your dog returns to you, as well as

77

making a great fuss of him, always make him sit and stay for a few seconds when he reaches you. This avoids the situation you often see when a dog returns beautifully but as the owner tries to get the lead on, the dog dances away and refuses to be caught. By making him sit and stay in front, you are putting yourself back in the controlling position, and giving yourself time to put him on the lead properly instead of allowing the situation to develop into a 'grab him quick' episode.

Your dog needs to accept other dogs and enjoy playing with them, but he still needs to come back to you the instant he is called. Not everyone will want your dog rushing up and charging about around their dogs, particularly if yours is a large, boisterous type, and you need to respect other people's wishes. Their dog may be recovering from an operation or just a bit nervous of other dogs, and their owners may feel protective towards them. The owners themselves may be nervous of other dogs, and they have every right to have their wishes respected. It is also very impressive if you can control your dog when the other party has not a hope of controlling theirs.

CHAPTER 8

Out and About

Respecting the Community

The next part of the process of obtaining the totally compatible community dog depends entirely on you and your attitudes. As a responsible dog owner, you must put your good intentions into practice.

Never allow your dog to foul footpaths, parks, recreational areas or in fact any public place. The easiest way to avoid this happening is to teach your dog to go on command (which you have already done) and to make him go at home. It is then quite easy to clean up after him, disposing of everything either via the manhole straight into the sewer system, or by wrapping up and disposing of it at the community tip. Another alternative is to install a 'dog loo' in your garden. These are on sale in most pet shops. The loo is a container, perforated at the base, which is buried in the garden. The excreta placed in it is broken down by the fluid which is obtained with the loo, and is then dispersed through the ground.

It is worth considering setting aside a small area of the garden for the dog's use. If this area is used from the very beginning, there is no difficulty in teaching him not to use other parts of the garden. Using similar principles to those employed in house-training, point and gently scold if he goes in the wrong place; praise when he does it right.

Bitches can ruin any lawn as their urine burns the grass; of course, male dogs will kill shrubs or trees that they continually use. The situation can be helped by dousing the area with water as soon as they relieve themselves. An ideal solution is to have the area that the dogs use covered with a layer of gravel, a minimum of 2 inches (5 cm) deep. The advantage with this method is that the area is then

The disposal problem. The dog loo is a very effective method of disposing of waste, which should be dropped into the unit. It is then dissolved by the chemical and dispersed safely into the ground.

well defined for the dog and will always look more attractive than what would eventually become a muddy patch. The area can then be frequently and easily bleached or disinfected to avoid any odour arising.

If your dog does foul any public area, it is your duty to clean up after him. This has now become the acceptable thing to do, and, thanks to many advertising and educational campaigns by several of the dog charities, no longer causes embarrassment to any conscientious dog owner. There are many types of scoopers available from pet stores, but quite frankly you need only take with you a supply of plastic carrier bags or similar. In most towns, you can be fined if you do let your dog foul the footpaths.

If your dog has to relieve himself when you are out, take him to an area away from any recreational facilities or groups of people. The edge of the park or field is suitable; if in town, teach him to go in the kerb. If you have a male dog, never let him cock his leg at every shop, lamp-post, tree, wall and so on. Service dogs and guide dogs would never do this, and there is no reason why yours should. It is just not necessary.

When walking with you along the street, your dog should always be on a lead and kept under control. He should walk close to you so that his lead does not trip or get tangled up with passers-by, and he should not be allowed to jump up or interfere with other people.

Dogs should never be taken into food shops or indeed any place where it is indicated that dogs are not allowed, whether you agree with it or not. There are usually Local Authority regulations in force regarding hygiene in places where food is sold and prepared, and you need to be aware of these. In fact, if you are going on a shopping trip, your dog is usually happier left at home, rather than having to struggle through crowds of people, especially on a hot day. If you do have to take him on a regular basis, he needs to learn to wait for you outside shops without making a noise. Once again, this is a situation where you will need to take time out on these trips for a specific training session to avoid bad habits creeping in. It is worth pointing out that this is a time when you will be glad you did not teach your dog to guard or be possessive, as he may well take the wrong attitude to people approaching him and the area where you have left him.

When out in the country, it is even more important that your dog is kept under control at all times. He must not be allowed to roam freely amongst livestock or in fields of crops and, of course, he must never ever be allowed to chase livestock or wild animals.

Travelling in Cars and Buses

One of the main pleasures of owning a dog is being able to take him out and about with you, and this will probably involve a good deal of travel in either cars or public transport.

If it appears your puppy is going to suffer from travel sickness, start to get him over this at an early age. Take him on very short journeys in the car to somewhere he enjoys going, say to the park. This should distract his attention from the car sickness. Have a game with him and then take the short journey home. You should gradually be able to increase the length of journeys he can tolerate. Do not sympathize too much with him as you will only exacerbate the problem. If the situation does not improve, try putting the dog on the floor in the front well of the passenger seat. Motion sickness is usually reduced if the outside movements cannot be seen. However, this should only be viewed as a short-term measure to solve this particular problem as it is not the safest way for your dog to travel. Once your dog is able to travel normally, you need to establish a safe routine.

It is vital that your dog does not learn bad habits to start with. It takes a dog no time at all

If your dog has to travel in a saloon-type car, he must learn to stay on the back seat. It is dangerous if he is allowed to jump about in the car.

Your dog should never be allowed to travel with his head out of the window. It is distracting to other drivers, and causes eye and ear problems for the dog.

to realize that when you are driving, there is absolutely no way that you can correct him or exert any control over him. Ideally the dog should travel in the back of either an estate or a hatchback car. If you have a saloon car, he needs to learn to travel on the back seat and stay there. It is extremely dangerous if he is allowed to jump about or be allowed to move about the car at will.

In order to stop him wandering about, tie his lead to a secure part of the car. If he is not allowed from the beginning to do his own thing he will not expect to be allowed to do it. Many types of dog-guards are available, and as well as stopping your dog creeping over to you, they also prevent a lot of dog hairs coming into the main body of the car, especially so with the mesh type of guard. They stop the dog leaning over the back seat and his tail swishing over the seats. If your dog has to travel on the back seat, you should not have the window down and allow him to travel with his head out of the window. As well as causing trouble to his eyes and ears, it is also very dangerous. He could try to jump out and your attention will need to be partly on him and not fully on your driving. It is also distracting to other drivers and users of the road.

One of the most difficult travelling problems to solve is noisiness. Many dogs can get very excited when they know they are going out to the park and, of course, while you are travelling, there is no way you can turn round to correct him. All your shouting will only exacerbate the situation. You will find that when you stop the car to correct him, he will stop barking; as soon as you start off again, he will resume it.

This is a situation that you really need to nip in the bud before it becomes established. As explained in earlier chapters, you will be teaching your dog to bark ('Speak') and cease on command and this is an excellent example of a situation where it can be used to great advantage. As soon as your puppy starts to make the slightest whine, give the command 'Quiet'. If the situation has already developed out of control, try not to take the dog where he is expecting to go every time. Take him on fruitless journeys where he does not get out

for a walk or see anybody, and then return straight home. Dogs are usually noisy in the car from sheer excitement, and if you make the journeys boring, the noise will stop, although obviously it will take quite a time for the habit to be erased.

This method can be speeded up using one of the modern personal alarms that are now readily available. These are small alarms that can be carried in your pocket or handbag, similar in size to a cigarette lighter. When pressed, they emit a high-pitched screech to frighten off any attacker. But for dog-training purposes, this high-pitched screech serves as an instant 'magic' reprimand for your dog. If he is being noisy, give the command 'Quiet' and, when he does not respond activate the alarm for just a short burst. The high pitch will

Do not let a 'catch me if you can' situation arise when letting your dog out of the car. You might miss.

have an immediate effect because a dog's hearing is sensitive to much higher sounds than ours is. He will soon learn that if he does not go quiet on command, there is an instant 'Act of God' reprimand. The advantage is that he does not associate the action with you at all. When he goes quiet, praise him. This method is very effective and does no actual harm to the dog's ears, other than cause momentary discomfort. In fact, many vets are now selling them as a training aid.

Your dog needs to be disciplined when getting out of the car. Very often, dogs just jump out of the car the second the door is opened and rush off, with their owners frantically trying to grab the lead. The dangers of this are obvious, and again, the right habits must be encouraged from the beginning. When the door is opened make your puppy 'Stay' until you get hold of his lead and then call him out. If you know he is going to try and jump out immediately you open the door, tie his lead to something rigid in the car when you put him in. This will prevent him jumping out until you are ready to release him and the bad habit cannot develop. Make him Sit and Stay until you have locked the car and *you* are ready to go.

If you are going to have to travel about by bus with your dog, again, do some short dummy runs during a quiet time of the day with the sole purpose of getting your puppy

Your dog should stay in the car until you are ready to get hold of his lead and let him out. Note the dog-guard and the boot bag, both worthwhile accessories to protect your car.

used to the experience. Just do a short journey first. On a double-decker bus, you will have to go upstairs with him and he will probably need encouraging up the stairs. He should lie on the floor by your seat. If he is happy to lie underneath it, so much the better, as he will then be completely out of the way and will not need to be disturbed by people passing by him. He must not be a nuisance to the other bus users and must not travel on the seat. It is not fair to expect other passengers to sit on a hair-covered seat later.

Training Clubs

A course at a local training club is an essential for your puppy. Even experienced trainers take their new puppies to a club as part of their socializing training. There are, however, no formal qualifications for setting up training clubs, and so there are good and bad. You need to scout around and visit a couple of clubs until you feel happy with one. Ask your vet for his recommendations as he will probably know most of your local clubs and will be seeing in his patients the results they are producing. He will probably be referring difficult canine clients to them in any case. Very often, local police-dog handlers run very successful pet-training clubs and a phone call to your local police station may be helpful. The Kennel Club produces a list of all training clubs that are registered with them, although a lot of very good pet-training clubs do not register with the Kennel Club. There is no

Dog club meetings are usually held indoors in local church halls, but if a club has the facility for outside training it can provide situations more like those you will meet when out with your dog. Here the dogs are trained to do heelwork approaching and passing other dogs and people. Eventually they will learn to ignore the approach of other people and dogs, and not pull towards them.

legal requirement for them to do so unless the club wishes to become competitive and start running shows and competitions under Kennel Club rules. This list may very well omit a very good pet club in your area.

When looking at a potential club, it is obviously important to see that the instructor is fully in control of the classes and able to handle any large boisterous or possibly aggressive dogs. You want to socialize your puppy and do not want him frightened at an early age. It is the instructor's responsibility to provide a safe environment for all the dogs in his class. The fact that someone may have trained an Obedience Champion does not necessarily mean he will make a good instructor. You need someone with a great deal of training experience with several breeds over several years. Ideally, try to find a club that puts on a specific puppy training course. These usually run for about six weeks and have the advantage over mixed-age classes of allowing your puppy to socialize first with other puppies of his age, avoiding the possible confrontations with older boisterous dogs that might worry him.

If a club says that there is a waiting list for twelve months or so, then you have to go elsewhere. You must socialize your puppy as soon as possible, and the very latest he should

A high degree of control. The handlers have left their dogs quite a distance away. The instructor is still keeping a close eye on things.

be attending a class is six months of age. Older than this and you are running the risk of his becoming more independent and out of control, making your training so much harder. The instructor should make the training as interesting and enjoyable to the dog as possible and try to simulate the situations you will meet outside.

Many clubs bore both dogs and handlers by doing heelwork round and round the perimeter of the hall week after week. The dogs find this very monotonous and although it may be necessary to start this way in order to teach the command 'Heel', the dogs soon need something more challenging. Look for an instructor who tries to be more innovative by having, for instance, two rows of dogs and handlers walking up and down the hall towards each other, passing in the middle or stopping to chat as they meet. Dogs soon learn to walk round a hall following the one in front, but the real test comes when they approach and face a dog coming towards them. After all, this is what will happen in the street. A good test for a dog is for him to try and do heelwork weaving in and out through a line of other dogs and their handlers. When it is your turn to be part of the line ensure that your dog stays sitting in the Heel position and ignores the moving dog.

Life is so much more peaceful for you if all your pets live in harmony!

Your instructor is not there to train your dog, he is there to train you to train your dog, and so it is important that he is someone you feel comfortable with and can listen to. Do not be put off by a chaotic, noisy first night of a training course. They always are! Stick with it and at the end of the course you will be astounded at the difference in the dogs and handlers. I often think we should video all first nights to show the handlers at the end of the course.

Having completed the introductory course, you are usually presented with a certificate, and some clubs even have a small competition with rosettes and prizes. You will usually have the opportunity to join one of the more ad-vanced classes, where you will start to have an insight into the fun that dog training really can be, and what an absorbing hobby it is.

Living With Other Pets and Livestock

If you are having to introduce your puppy to an already-established family cat, be prepared to have a sulky cat for a few weeks. Provided you do not force any face-to-face confrontations, it should not take the cat too long to come round to accepting your puppy, if not actually liking the new addition, but he has to do it in his own time. Make sure the cat has an easily

There is no reason why your dog cannot co-exist with wild animals. He should not be encouraged to chase livestock or any living creature.

accessible, comfortable place that he can reach and the puppy cannot. When the two do actually meet face to face, the cat is usually able to hold his own and take good care of himself. Your puppy must never be encouraged to chase the cat as he meanders about the house and garden, and he must be severely reprimanded if he does.

Other people love and cherish their pets as much as you do your own and your dog has no right to chase any other cats, even if they do come into your garden. Do not use your dog as a garden guardian. You may find the situation could backfire on you when he is older. He will enjoy the thrill of the chase and will be oblivious to all your attempts to stop him, temporarily forgetting rules regarding the flower-beds. A dog in full flight can do an awful lot of damage very quickly, and think what could happen if he spies a cat when he is out for a walk.

If you live in or near the country, it is important that your dog also learns not to chase livestock and other farm or wild animals. When you have the opportunity, walk your dog, on a lead, past fields of sheep, cows and horses. He will probably be curious, so allow him to sniff and investigate but stop him immediately if he starts to lunge or bark at the animals. Also, endeavour to find groups of ducks and chickens to help in his education and learning of the Country Code.

CHAPTER 9

Training after Six Months of Age

By the age of six months, your puppy will be ready to take on the more formal training that he needs. Although he is already behaving acceptably in most of the everyday situations you find yourselves in together, most dogs benefit from the extra mental stimulation that further training gives them. You will also learn to understand your dog better and, in fact, the more training you do, the closer the bond between you will become. It only takes a few minutes a day while you are out for your walk. Lengthy sessions will only bore the dog and become tedious for both of you.

When starting to teach any of these new exercises, try to find an area, such as the park or open land, where there are as few distractions as possible, but where you have plenty of room to be able to play and run about with your dog during the training. The important thing to remember is to make all the sessions fun and enjoyable for the dog, so that he wants to work with you. There is no pleasure in trying to motivate a dog who hates every minute of his training.

Heelwork

This subject has already been covered briefly in Chapter 7 (*see* page 69). It is one of the first exercises you can start to teach your dog. Once

The perfect stylish heelwork position. Note the handler is holding the dog's ball to get his head looking up. The dog is working happily with his tail up and wagging.

your dog has become practised in basic heelwork, you can introduce additional commands that will enable you to improve your standard and achieve a certain polish.

Your first aim is to have him walking beside you with his shoulder close to and level with your left knee. The lead should be loose, that is, with no jerking or physically holding him in position with it. He should be aware of your movements and follow you closely through a variety of twists and turns, always staying in the same position at your side, and when you halt he should automatically sit at your side and wait until you walk off again. He should pay full attention to you, work in a happy manner and will look at his most stylish when he is actually looking up at you.

One of the biggest obstacles to overcome in teaching heelwork is keeping the dog's attention on you in the first place. Very often people try to teach heelwork with the dog looking every which way but at them. The frustrated owner has to resort to shouting, nagging and jerking the dog with little real effect and all they will eventually achieve is a bored, unhappy and confused partner.

Before actually starting heelwork as an exercise, it is a good idea to teach your dog to watch you and to enjoy doing so, and the best way to achieve this is to make yourself interesting to him. When out for a walk do not always let him meander off doing his own thing sniffing and snooping around, but change direction and run off from him, sometimes hide from him. Have his toy with you and have fun with him, play with him, holding it high to encourage him to look up at you. Occasionally, perhaps, give him titbits. Do anything to make him aware of you and know that you are fun to be with, and that you are unpredictable. When he is at the stage where he is always looking at you to see what you will be up to next, you are then ready to proceed on to heelwork training.

Use the same type of collar that you have found suitable in teaching him to walk properly along the streets (*see* Chapter 7, page 69). Start with him sitting at your left-hand side, close to and square with your left leg. Hold the lead in your right hand so that it loops down just below the dog's head. Any longer than that and you will not be able to use it to control him, and it will get in the way; any shorter and you will be keeping him in position only by physically holding him there. He has to learn to stay at heel of his own accord.

Make sure you have the dog's attention before starting off. Click your fingers or use his name. When you are ready, give his name and the command 'Close' and step off smartly

This puppy is being encouraged to bounce along at the handler's side from a very young age. No formal training is necessary at this age, but the dog is enjoying looking up and wondering what his 'mum' is going to do next. Getting the dog's attention is one of the biggest obstacles to overcome when teaching formal heelwork.

When teaching heelwork, remember to break off and play with him at intervals. You must avoid boredom setting in.

and confidently with no hesitation. If your dog's preliminary training in watching you has been well done, you will probably find he will walk to heel quite naturally with his head up looking at you. If he does so, praise him lavishly, carry on for a few yards only, then release and have a game with him.

If he does not follow you immediately give a quick jerk on the lead to get his attention and do everything you can to encourage him. You must keep walking; do not stop and wait for your dog. He has to learn to follow you, not the other way round. If you hesitate and wait for him, he will never get up. Keep all your commands very light-hearted with the emphasis at this stage on jollying him along and making everything fun.

Walk for only ten yards in a straight line in these early sessions and then release and have a game with him. Each time he wanders away from you, encourage him back to heel with the command 'Close' given crisply and clearly each time, followed by praise. If the voice alone does not work, give a short jerk on the lead. The lead must not stay taut at any time as the dog will only pull against it to get away from it. If he seems really reluctant to start heelwork in these early stages, then try to encourage him by holding his toy or a titbit in your left hand.

It is far better to encourage him like this than to nag him and perhaps put him off for life. There is no need at this stage to expect him to sit when you halt; this will be taught

91

Lead control for putting the dog into the Sit when you halt. The lead is held loosely in the right hand while doing heelwork.

As you approach a halt, the lead needs to be shortened to give you control of his front end. Start by putting your left hand on his lead down near the collar.

later when he has more idea of what you are actually requiring of him. After a short game, repeat the process again. Do it only a few times each session to avoid any boredom creeping in. When he seems to understand what you are expecting of him, add some interest by putting in some twists and turns to keep him on his toes. Try about-turns (that is, turning 180 degrees and going back the way you came), right-and-left turns. If he has a tendency to work wide, away from your leg, walk in large right-hand circles which encourage him to walk in closer to you. Before making a turn, give him some warning by saying his name and giving the command 'Close'. Try varying your speed and if he is slow and inclined to lag

behind you, break into a run. If you slow up for him he will just go slower and slower.

When he is happily and competently walking to heel, you can introduce the Sit when you halt. In the early stages, this requires a good deal of lead control, and you may need to practise this on your own without your dog so that you do not worry him. During heelwork, the lead should be held in the right hand. As you approach a halt, put your left hand on the lead near to the collar. Pass this into the right hand (you now have in effect a short lead giving you control of his head and front end); at the same time, stop walking, give the command 'Sit', and push the dog into the sit with your left hand. Then praise him.

Use your left hand to gather up the lead into the right hand. You now have a short lead, with your left hand free to push him into the Sit. This is all done while you are still in motion.

As you halt, push him into the Sit position, close and square to the left leg.

By having control of his head, you should be able to push his rear into the Sit in the correct position, as he was at the beginning of the exercise, that is, close and square to your leg. Eventually, you will find he will automatically go into the Sit as you halt, and you need not even give the command.

Gradually, he will be able to concentrate for longer periods and you can increase both the amount of heelwork in any one session and the complexity. Try to keep him interested and alert and always stop any session before he gets bored. It is a great feeling to have a dog working with you as part of a team, a dog that is both happy and stylish, and it is in the heelwork that this can really be shown impressively.

The Stay Exercises

Having already learnt the meaning of the 'Stay' command you are now ready to build this up to the stage where you will be able to leave your dog in the Sit, Down or Stand position, gradually building up both time and distance away from him, until you are even able to leave him out of sight, confident in the knowledge that he will not move until you return to him.

The Stay should be one of the easiest exercises to teach a dog, as it does not actually require any thought or conscious actions on his behalf. He has only to remain in one spot until told to do otherwise. However, so often

93

things seem to go drastically wrong and it is unfortunate that once this exercise has gone wrong it is so very difficult to correct it. The secret of achieving an absolutely reliable Stay is to take the training literally one step at a time, and resist the temptation to progress faster than the dog is capable of.

The Sit-Stay

Your puppy has already been taught to sit and stay at your side until you are ready to release him, and he should now be quite steady at this. Only progress on to the next stage once he is absolutely reliable and makes no attempt to move until you praise and release him. If he is still fidgety, persevere, making him sit and stay at your side, and make no attempt yet to try to move away from him. Always anticipate his moving and have your hand ready to push him back in to the Sit before he can actually get up.

As he gets steadier, increase the time he has to stay a little at a time. Do not be tempted to be too ambitious and leave him so long that he actually does get up. You are then taking a backward step in his training: the more times he gets up, the more of a habit it becomes for him to do so. Only when he will stay at your side with no attempts at moving until you tell

The Sit-Stay. With the dog at the Heel position, give the command 'Stay'. A hand signal often helps to reinforce the command.

Very carefully, watching the dog all the time, take one small step to the right. If the dog looks as if he is going to move, be ready to push him back in to the Sit position. You should be quick enough to prevent him getting up at all.

him to do so, are you ready to move on to the next stage.

With the dog on the lead in the Sit at your side give the command 'Stay' very clearly and take one small step to the right. At this short distance away, you are still close enough to enforce the command if necessary. Watch your dog all the time and if he should attempt to move, push him into the Sit in order to prevent him from doing so. If your preparation has been done correctly he will not attempt to move. Stay away for just a few seconds, then step back to his side. Do not let him get up immediately, stand at his side for a few seconds and then release and praise him in the usual way. By having a definite cut-off point for the exercise, you will avoid his getting into the habit of getting up to greet you as you return to him. If, when you leave him, he looks fidgety, keep saying 'Stay'. Avoid using the dog's name as this will encourage him to come to you.

When you are sure that he will stay when you step away to the side, you can start leaving him by walking forward from him. This is more difficult as the dog is more inclined to follow you as you walk forward, and he might also think that he is going to be doing heel-work. It is important that you leave him in no doubt as to what you require and give clear

Do not stay away from him for too long. Watch him at all times.

Return to his side. Praise him but do not release him straight away; wait a few seconds first.

Gradually build up the Stay until you can lay the lead on the ground. The next time, he should be able to stay off the lead.

commands before you actually step off to avoid any confusion setting in. Give the command 'Stay', step off, and turn and face him, watching him all the time. Return to his side as before, then release and praise him. At this stage, the dog is still on the lead and you will gradually build up the distance you leave him, until you are at the end of the lead. Make sure you do not tug or pull on the lead while he is still learning to stay.

Once he is confident and staying 100 per cent of the time, you can dispense with the lead altogether. Command 'Stay', walk away to the end of the lead and turn to face him. When he is looking steady, lay the lead on the ground, saying 'Stay' as you do so. If he is still reliable, next time you leave him, unobtrusively take off his lead.

Gradually build up both the length of time you leave him and the distance. Only increase one at a time and if at any stage the dog breaks the Stay, go back a stage to consolidate. The secret of this exercise is never to let the dog break the Stays by jumping the stages and progressing too quickly.

As his confidence grows, try to cut down the number of times you are saying 'Stay' to him. Eventually you should need only to say 'Stay' as you leave him and nothing else until you release and praise him.

Putting the dog into the Down position. Start with him sitting at your side. Give the command 'Down', pull down with his lead and push downwards and outwards on his shoulders.

The pressure on his shoulders will unbalance him and he should gently go into the Down position.

The Down-Stay

The easiest way to get your dog into the Down is to start with him in the sitting position at your side. Adjust his collar so that the lead is hanging directly under his chin. Holding the lead with your right hand, pull downwards while at the same time push gently downwards and slightly sidewards and backwards with your left hand just behind his shoulder blades. This will unbalance him slightly and he should slide into the Down quite easily. At the same time, give a clear firm command 'Down'.

Try not to make sudden movements or be too forceful when pushing him down, as he will worry and set himself against you by stiffening his front legs and struggling away from you. If this does happen, you will need to kneel beside him, putting your left hand over

When he is down, praise him and keep your hand near his shoulders so you can keep him down if he tries to jump up.

The 'lion lay'. It takes only one quick movement for the dog to be up and away.

his shoulders to hold his left leg and, with your right hand holding his other leg, gently lift his front legs. At the same time, gently roll him over by pushing down on his shoulders with your left arm.

When he is in the Down, keep your hand on his shoulders praising him and saying 'Down' all the time. When he feels relaxed and shows no indication of attempting to get up, take your hand away and start to stand up saying 'Stay' as you do so. As with the Sit, be prepared for him to move and make sure you are quick enough to anticipate this and place your hand back on his shoulders to keep him in the Down. If you find a real problem in keeping him down while you try to stand up, put his lead on the ground and put your foot on it to restrain him as he tries. Do not make the lead too tight as he will fight against it, but it should be short enough to prevent him from standing up as you rise.

Once you are able to stand up by his side, keep him in the Down for a few seconds then release and praise him. Only release him when he is staying correctly, even if it is only for a few seconds. Do not release him because he is getting up anyway of his own accord; make him stay for a few seconds more. When he is in the Down, push his haunches over so that he is not in the lion position (hind legs tucked squarely underneath him). The lion position needs only one spring for him to be up and

Push the dog's rear end over. He now has to make two movements to get up, giving you more time to intercept him if he tries to break the Down.

away, but if you have pushed his haunches over, he will need two movements to get up, thus giving you more time.

You can now proceed in exactly the same way as the Sit-Stay advancing literally just a step at a time, and always going back to consolidate a stage if the dog shows signs of confusion or defiance.

The Stand-Stay

The principles for teaching the Stand-Stay are exactly the same as for the Sit- and Down-Stays once you have taught your dog the command 'Stand'. There are two ways to approach this, and you will soon find out the method that suits your dog best. The Stand needs to be taught very gently, because if a dog gets worried, he will just sink or collapse into the Sit or Down positions. The dog has to learn to stay in the Stand without moving his front feet forward. With your dog in the usual position in the Sit at heel, run your left hand along his side gently going under his tummy to encourage him to go into the Stand by bringing his hind legs up. His front legs should remain in the same place. Be very careful not to grab at his tummy, or pull him up by grabbing a handful of hair.

The action is a gentle lifting one. The

The Stand-Stay. Start with the dog in the Sit, run your hand along his side, gently going under his tummy to raise him up. You need to use a soft voice to command him 'Stand', as any harshness will make him collapse into the Sit or Down.

When he is up, make sure he is standing comfortably or he will move as you leave him. The Stand-Stay is the most difficult to teach and has to be taken very slowly.

command 'Stand' should be given in a soft, gentle, higher-pitched voice than the one you use for the more authoritative 'Sit' or 'Down' commands. Some dogs do seem to worry about being handled into the Stand and if this appears to be the case, the second method may suit him better. Walk him slowly forward on the lead a few paces, then as you stop, again gently run your hand along his side slightly underneath his tummy to prevent him going into the Sit. As you do this, gently give the command 'Stand'. When doing this, avoid going into proper heelwork as you move forward. This will only confuse him as you are already teaching him to go automatically into the Sit when you halt on heelwork. Just walk him around casually. Once you have him happily standing, then proceed in exactly the same way as the Sit- and Down-Stays.

The Recall

The Recall is broken down into four separate components: the Wait, the Call-up, the Present (facing you in the Sit), and the Finish. The complete exercise consists of your leaving the dog in the Sit and walking a few yards from him, turning and facing him. On the command 'Come' (the Call-up) the dog comes briskly and sits in front of you (the Present).

On the command 'Heel' the dog walks round behind your back into the Sit at the Heel position (the Finish). At all times, the dog should be happy to run to you and, therefore, it is often sensible to perfect the Present and Finish as separate exercises. This will avoid the dog becoming worried about the actual Call-up, which he may do if each time he reaches you he is nagged about the accuracy of the Sit and Finish.

The Wait

Before starting to teach the Recall, your dog should be doing a reliable Sit-Stay. Great care must now be taken not to undo this Stay training, which could well happen if when starting to teach the Recall, you call the dog to you each and every time you leave him. The Stay must continue to be reinforced. As usual, your dog will be on the lead when you start training the Recall. It is important for this exercise that the lead is at least 3 feet (92 cm) long. Tell your dog 'Wait' and leave him. Walk to the end of the lead, turn and face him. Then return to his side and praise him, but do not let him get up. Using the command 'Wait' can help to differentiate between the Stay where he has to stay put no matter what. The 'Wait' command means he waits until told to do something else. Repeat this part of the exercise – leaving and returning to him – several

The Wait. Command 'Stay', and go to the end of the lead.

The Call-up. As you call him, run backwards to encourage him to run to you. Put him in the Sit as he reaches you.

times. Call him up to you only once every four or five times. This way you are continuing to reinforce the Stay exercise.

The Call-Up and Present

Leave the dog in the Sit, give the command 'Wait' and go to the end of the lead; turn and face him. Using his name plus the command 'Come', start running backwards. As the dog comes towards you gather up the lead, so that by the time he reaches you, you are holding the lead close to his collar. You then have control of his front end so you can lean over and push him into the Sit remembering to give the

command 'Sit'. Praise him, keep him sitting there for a few moments, then release him and have a game. It is important that the dog thinks the Recall is fun and that he enjoys running to you.

For the perfect Present your dog will be sitting centrally in front of you, not to the right or left. He should also be reasonably close to you. Practise getting him to sit in the right position in front by teaching this separately. Put the dog in the Sit (on the lead of course), tell him to 'Wait' and then stand about a yard (1 m) just in front of him. Stand either slightly to the right or to the left of him and guide him into the right position in front of you, using his

The correct Present position. The dog is sitting centrally to the handler, not to the right or left.

name and the command 'Come'. He will soon learn exactly what you require of him, and will start to place himself correctly in front of you.

When your dog is doing the Call-up instantly and reliably, without any physical handling or help from you, or guidance with the lead, you can progress to trying the Recall off the lead. The first time you take the lead off, try to do so quietly and unobtrusively, after having already done a couple of Recalls on the lead as normal first. When the lead is off, you will find that your dog will automatically Recall as before, but if he should run off or not respond quickly enough, immediately put him

back on the lead. Leave it a few more sessions before you try him off the lead again.

The Finish

Put the dog in the Sit and stand in front of him so that he is in the Present position. On the command 'Heel' you want the dog to go round behind you, keeping close to your legs, and finish up sitting in the Heel positon at your left-hand side.

Eventually, he will do this while you remain stationary, but initially you will have to put in some movement in order to encourage him to get up and move round. If you try to pull him round from the Sit he will resent this and pull against you. With him in the Present position, take the lead in your right hand, take a step backwards with your right foot only, and at the same time saying 'Heel'. As your dog gets up guide him round the back with the lead, which you then pass into your left hand. As you do this, step forward again with your right foot back to the original position. As your dog reaches the Heel position tell him to 'Sit' and if necessary push him into the Sit in the normal way. Praise, release and have a game with him. Once he understands what you are asking of him, you can remain stationary while he goes round to heel. Only when he has mastered each of the separate components of the Recall should you put them altogether.

The Retrieve

When it comes to teaching the Retrieve, it is very much easier if you have a dog who already enjoys chasing after things and bringing them back to you. Playing with your puppy and encouraging him to pick things up is an important part of your pre-retrieve training. However, when it comes to teaching the Retrieve properly, it needs to be taught as a formal exercise to be performed on command. A dog

The Finish. Teach this as a separate exercise to begin with. Start with the dog in the Present position.

To get the dog up and moving, take one step backwards with your right leg. This avoids your having to drag or jerk the dog up. Guide him round the back of you.

As the dog goes round, pass the lead behind your back from your right to your left hand.

As the dog comes round to heel, step forward with your right leg, back to your original position, and pass the lead to your right hand. Put the dog in the Sit at Heel.

who is taught Retrieve only as a play exercise, will sooner or later turn round and decide he does not want to play that game anymore, and there will be nothing you can do about it.

If he does not take the article straight away you will need to open his jaws and place the article in his mouth being careful not to hurt him. The easiest way to get him to open his mouth is to put your hand over his muzzle and gently press his jowls near his back teeth. As you press against his teeth, his mouth will open and you can then gently pop the article in his mouth praising him and saying 'Hold'. He will probably struggle to spit it out, but hold it in for a few seconds then say clearly 'Leave'

and take it out. He must be allowed to let it go only on your command, but if you are losing control and he does spit it out, make sure he hears the command 'Leave' loudly and clearly as he does so. With a lot of patience and practice, he will soon learn to take the article on the command 'Hold'.

When your dog is happily taking the article each time you present it to him, hold it a few inches from him so that he has to move his head forward to take it. You may have to gently push his head forward the first few times. Gradually increase the distance he has to move until you have the article on the floor and he will pick it up on the command 'Hold'. At

When starting the Retrieve, use a soft article that cannot accidently hurt him. Encourage him to hold it; if necessary, open his mouth and place the article in to it.

Do not let him spit the article out until you command him to. While you are holding it in his mouth, give the command 'Hold'.

this stage, with him on the lead, start to take a few paces backwards away from him after he has picked it up saying 'Fetch' getting him to bring the article to you. Do not worry about making him sit at this stage, but take the article from him saying 'Leave'. Make sure he does not spit it out at your feet. Gradually introduce the Sit in front, making him hold the article until he has sat and you have told him to leave. Remember the praise.

Once he has learnt to hold on command and has the idea of the bringing and presenting the article to you, you can start putting the whole exercise together. As usual, start with the dog on his lead, sitting at the Heel posi-

tion. Tell him to 'Wait' and throw the article just about the length of the lead in front of you. Give the command 'Fetch' and encourage the dog to go forward to pick up the article. You will probably need to step forward to encourage him towards the article and then point to it. If he does not pick it up immediately give the command 'Hold' and push his head down gently to pick it up. If the preliminary training has been done correctly, he should pick it up on the command 'Hold' without any problem.

As he picks it up, run backwards, encouraging him to you; as you stop he should automatically go into the Present position in front of you. Take the article from him on the

Gradually move the article further away so that the dog has to move his head forward. You may need to assist and push him!

Eventually the article will be on the floor in front of the dog.

Note the dog is still on the lead. As you tell him 'Fetch', take him forward to the article. If he will not pick it up straight away, use the command 'Hold', which he is now familiar with.

When he has picked it up, run backwards so that he runs towards you with the article.

command 'Leave'. Do not let him drop it of his own accord. The exercise is then completed with the finish to Heel, as in the Recall. The final stage is to remove the lead and increase the distance you throw the article. As usual, when trying anything off the lead for the first time, do a couple of training retrieves first on the lead, and then remove the lead quietly and unobtrusively.

The Retrieve is an exercise that needs enthusiasm from the dog, and you must be careful not to lose this in the early stages by being too finicky about the accuracy of each part of the exercise. In the very early stages, if the dog is inclined to rush out straight away for the article without waiting for the command 'Fetch' do not worry too much. This is a good fault. It is far better to have this, than a dog who is reluctant and creeps out slowly to the article.

The Wait can be perfected at a later stage, once he is fully competent on the Retrieve. There are several ways of doing this and usually a combination of them all works best. First, hold on to the dog's collar when you throw the article and keep saying 'Wait' to him. On the command 'Fetch', release him. Second, throw the article, holding his collar if necessary, and then before sending him to fetch it, walk around him once. When his Wait is slightly more reliable, go out yourself and retrieve the article occasionally. What you are doing is keeping him alert and actually thinking about the Wait – he is not always sure if he is going to be sent or not.

The retrieve article you are using should never be left with the dog as a play article, or just used as a toy to throw on his walks. It should be kept specifically for his retrieve training. The article usually used in competition is a dumb-bell, so as soon as he is happy holding the article you have used to start him off, transfer over to a dumb-bell. Start by teaching him to hold it correctly; it has to be held by the dowel and not by the ends. Make

sure the dumb-bell is a suitable size for him. He could catch his mouth on the corners if it is too small, and once this happens he will be very reluctant to fetch it again. If a dumb-bell is too large, it makes it very uncomfortable for the dog to fetch and to sit in front of you correctly.

The Instant Down

The ability to make your dog Down on command from a distance is a valuable asset to you. In fact, it can prove to be a life-saver if a dog who is in full flight, heading towards a busy road, can be dropped instantly.

Training begins when the dog has mastered the 'Down' command at your side. The next stage is to start making him obey when he is further away from you, and this is taught very much like a game. Have the dog on the lead and run about playing with him. At a moment when he is at the end of the lead, shout out clearly 'Down' and at the same time jerk the lead down towards the ground. When he is down, go up to him, praise him and carry on with the game. Keep repeating this frequently, as long as it is treated as a game, the dog should not get bored.

When he is going down instantly and quickly, try taking the lead off (immediately after doing a few practice ones on the lead). When he is further from you again, shout out 'Down' and this time point to the ground to reinforce the command. When he is down go up to him, praise and release him. Avoid calling the dog to you after he has gone down, or using his name when giving him the 'Down' command, because he may get into the habit of creeping towards you before going down and you want him to go down at the exact spot you commanded him. The command has to be loud and really clear so that he is in no doubt as to your requirements, even at long distances.

Gradually increase his distance from you over a period of weeks. At the first sign of disobedience or slowness in obeying the command, immediately go straight back to the beginning, putting him back on the lead. This is an exercise where he can easily learn that when you are away from him, he does not have to obey because you are not in a position to enforce the command. By going back to basics the very first time he even thinks of defying you, you are leaving him in no doubt that this will not be allowed. You must not let the idea that he can do as he pleases the chance to get firmly implanted in his mind.

CHAPTER 10

Entering Competitions

Types of Show

Exemption Shows

Having followed the training through to this stage, you might want to have a go at a few competitions, and Exemption Shows are the ideal place to start. As their name suggests, these shows are exempt from the normal rules and regulations laid down by the Kennel Club and are in fact very informal events. They are usually held in conjunction with fêtes, gymkhanas or other fund-raising events, and very often all the proceeds are for local charities. Advertisements for them can be found in pet shop windows, vet's surgeries or your local paper. They are a lot of fun and a good day out for all the family.

Entries for these shows are taken on the day, and it is not necessary for dogs to be registered with the Kennel Club. The obedience classes do not require the absolute precision of the top-flight competitive events so if you have trained your dog to the standard described in this book, he will be capable of entering and having some chance of success in the starter classes.

Invariably, there are novelty classes to be entered, such as, 'The Dog who looks Most Like its Owner', 'The Dog with the Waggiest Tail', and 'The Dog with the Most Appealing Eyes', as well as perhaps junior handling classes. If your dog is a pedigree, there are often beauty classes scheduled as well.

As the shows are exempt from Kennel Club rules, the organizing committee can choose the exercises they wish to include in any class and even what the classes will actually be called, so be prepared for slight differences in the schedules for each show. However, you can be assured there will be a class your dog can enter. The starter class usually only includes heelwork on the lead, a Recall (either on or off the lead), and a Sit- or Down-Stay. Remember that these shows are designed for fun and cater for people and dogs who have never been to a show before.

The advertisement will tell you the time that entries will be taken from. You should arrive soon after that time and go to the table where the entries are being collected. It is usually quite chaotic, but take time to study the schedule, choose all the classes you want to enter, fill in the entry form and hand it in, together with your entry fees.

Next, find the ring where the judges for your first class will commence. The obedience tests run for most of the day as each dog is judged individually in the ring, with the exception of the Stay exercise, where all the dogs in the class are called in the ring together. Make sure you find out the time of the Stays so that you do not miss them.

When it is your turn to go in for your individual work, there will be two other people in the ring: the judge and the steward. The steward will put you at your ease, tell you exactly what to do and direct you around the ring.

When you enter the ring, the steward will put you at ease and tell you exactly what to do. Note the master scoreboard at the side of the ring.

The first exercise is usually heelwork. The steward will tell you where to start from and everything after that is performed on his command. Make sure your dog is sitting nice and square beside you to start with, and that you have a loose lead.

On the steward's command 'Forward', step off confidently with your dog, making sure to give him the command 'Heel' clearly. Try to talk and act towards your dog exactly as you do when training him, but this is easier said than done. It is so easy to be almost frozen stiff with fear as the nerves and butterflies in the stomach take control. During the heelwork, the steward will give the commands 'Right turn', 'Left turn' and 'About turn', and you should make sure these are sharp 90 degree and 180 degree turns. On the command 'Halt', ensure you give a clear command 'Sit'.

The judge will be looking to see what the dog is able to do on his own and you should not be actually handling your dog at all. Any touching of the dog, or jerking and tightening of the lead will cause points to be deducted. You can, however, use your voice and hand signals as much as you like, so make full use of this, giving your dog plenty of encouragement all the time. You can also slap your leg or clap you hands together to get his attention.

A common fault when people enter the ring for the first few times is to lose confidence in their dog, and not believe he can really do it. They walk slower and slower until the dog just stops moving at all. If you think you are losing the dog and he is lagging behind you, walk faster. The brisker you are, the more alert the dog will be. At the end of the exercise, the steward will say 'Exercise finished', and then you can really praise and play with your dog.

The next exercise will probably be the Recall and this is done just as in training. Tell your dog to 'Wait' and on the steward's command, leave him. The steward will tell you how far to go and when to call him. Remember to use your voice and hand signals to encourage him in. Tell him to sit in front, without touching him, and then finish, again on the steward's command. If you are not very confident that your dog will stay when you are walking away from him, do not forget that you can talk to him all the time. Keep saying 'Wait' to him as you are walking away.

Another exercise he might be asked to perform is a temperament test. For this, your dog will have to stand beside you while the judge approaches and strokes him. The dog should show no signs of either aggression or nervousness. If you think this may prove a problem, practise it with various people prior to the show.

The Stay exercises are the only ones where you are not allowed to talk to your dog all the time. All entrants will be called into the ring at the same time and will be placed around the edge of the ring. When everybody is ready, the steward will give the command 'Last commands' when you will tell your dog to 'Stay'. If you say anything after this, you will be penalized. You will be told to leave your dog and go to the centre of the ring. At the end of the

The Down-Stay in progress in the ring.

specified time, the steward will tell you to return to your dog. Go back to his side at the Heel position. He should still stay there and only when the steward says 'Exercise finished' can you praise and release him.

At the end of your test, the judge will tell you what you have lost points for and will probably give you helpful hints as to how to remedy them. A lot of the faults will be due to your own nervousness, but this is something everyone has gone through. The points will be entered on the master scoreboard at the side of the ring and during the day you can keep a check of your progress in the class. There are usually plenty of rosettes on offer and with a bit of luck, one might well be yours.

Open and Championship Obedience Shows

If you have had some success at the Exemp-
tion Shows, you may well decide that you would like to go one stage further and enter some Open or Championship Obedience Shows. These shows are held under Kennel Club rules and regulations and are, therefore, more organized than Exemption Shows.

The entries are always taken in advance, usually about a month before the date of the show, and the entry has to be made on an official entry form obtainable from the secretary of the organizing society. The shows are advertised in one of the specialist magazines, which are not available through newsagents, but by subscription only. The two current ones are *Dog Training Weekly* and *The Obedience Competitor* and you may well have already seen them at your dog club or at one of the shows you have attended. A subscription to one of them is essential as they are your only source of information on when shows are being held, when entries are closing and

One of the beauty classes being judged. The judge is examining the Golden Retriever.

where to obtain schedules. They also contain judges' critiques on the winning dogs.

Before you can enter, your dog has to be registered by name at the Kennel Club. If you have a pedigree dog, this may already have been done by the breeder and all you will need to do is complete a 'transfer of ownership' form obtainable from either the breeder or Kennel Club. A crossbreed will also need to be registered and again the relevant form is available from the Kennel Club. It can be fun choosing a competition name for your dog.

Open Shows held under Kennel Club rules have available five classes that can be scheduled and, unlike Exemption Shows, the classes are well defined and there can be no alterations to them. The five classes are, from the lowest, Beginners, Novice, Test A, Test B and Test C. Beginners and Novice actually consist of almost the same exercises. There are only two differences in these two classes, the first being that only handlers who have never won a total of two or more first prizes previously (excluding prizes won at Exemption Shows) can enter. Experienced handlers starting off a new dog would have to enter Novice, so if you are inexperienced, you will enter the Beginners class where you will have to compete only with competitors like yourself. The second difference is that Novice includes a temperament test.

The Beginners Test consist of:

1. Heel on Lead   15 points
2. Heel Free   20 points
3. Recall and Finish   10 points
4. Retrieve   25 points
5. Sit (1 minute, handler in
   sight)   10 points
6. Down (2 minutes, handler in
   sight)   20 points
   _____
                                 100 points
   _____

'Who's a clever girl then'. The end of a successful day.

As with Exemption Shows, you can talk to and encourage your dog all the time, with the exception of the Stay exercises.

If you are considering entering regularly you will need to look around for a competitive training club to join. Many pet-training clubs do not have a competitive section and you will need this for several reasons. First, if other members are attending shows regularly, they will be able to help you through the procedures of the first few shows. Also, it is so much nicer to see and be able to meet up with some familiar faces at the shows. Second, as you progress through the classes, there are certain exercises that you will need help with and cannot train for on your own, notably Scent Discrimination. If your pet club cannot help, take note of the societies advertising in *Dog Training Weekly* and approach them. Even if there is not one in your area the secretary will know of all the competitive clubs near you and will be able to put you in touch with them.

This chapter will have given you an insight into how to get started on the competitive side of dog training. If you really get involved it is a very rewarding, albeit time-consuming, hobby, but there is an awful lot more to learn. The scope of this book does not extend to cover the techniques and technicalities involved in serious competitive training, but if you have followed the methods used in this book for the basic training of your puppy, you should have no problem in progressing with him. Your new-found friends will be your source of information and encouragement, and one day you may well be driving home from a show, the proud owner of a new Obedience Champion.

CHAPTER 11

Advanced Training

The following exercises are included as they are fun to teach and will give you a better idea of what it is possible to achieve with a well-trained dog. However, if you are thinking of taking up obedience competitions as a serious hobby, you would be well advised to join a competitive club to cover the more technical aspects of the exercises needed for success in the obedience ring.

The Sendaway

Before starting the Sendaway you should have already mastered the Instant Down, as outlined in Chapter 9 (*see* page 109). There is little point in being able to send your dog away from you to any designated place if you are unable to control him once he is there.

Up to this point, all the formal exercises have consisted of either keeping the dog with you, or getting him to come to you. You are now going to start sending him away from you and you need to find an easy way of getting this message across to him.

There are many ideas and methods in current use, but one of the easiest is to get him initially to run to and lay on some sort of mat, a remnant of carpet is ideal. Start with a largish square that is big enough for the dog to lie on; as the training progresses the mat should be cut down in size. The first stage is to get him used to lying on this mat indoors. Put it in the place where he normally lies, or on his bed.

When he is quite happy being sent to this mat indoors, you can start on the Sendaway exercise.

Put the mat a couple of feet (60 cm) in front of you, and with the dog on the lead sitting at Heel, point his head towards the mat. He needs to get used to his head being handled and pointed towards the mat, as this is important in the latter stages of the exercise. He should not object as he will be able to see the mat and will be looking towards it in any case, but if he does fight against the handling, persevere gently. When he is looking straight ahead, give the command 'Away', run up to the mat with him, command 'Down', and then praise and release him.

Practise this several times each session and over the period of a few weeks, gradually increase the distance that the mat is away from you. When he is confidently running out on the lead, dispense with it on the odd occasion. As he can still see the mat, he should run out with no hesitation. When you have dropped him, always walk up to him and praise him. Do not call him back to you at this stage as you could encourage him to anticipate this and he will either not go down at all or start creeping back to you before he drops.

When he is running out to his mat over a reasonable distance, you can start to make the mat smaller. Eventually, it will be so small that he will only see it as he approaches it. At this stage, you can dispense with it altogether as your dog will now have learnt that if he runs

The Sendaway. Pointing the dog towards a marked 'box' similar to those used in competitive obedience.

Running the dog up and dropping him in the box.

The dog is at a more advanced stage and can now be sent on his own. The handler is assisting him by giving a hand signal as the dog is sent.

away from you in a straight line he will eventually reach the piece of mat. You are now in the position to send him and drop him to nothing in any direction you point him. He will run away from you and keep going until he is told to 'Down'. To finish the exercise, approach him, praise and release him.

His confidence should be growing all the time, but if at any time he starts hesitating, revert to using the mat immediately. Only send him in one direction on any one training session. If you try to send him to another point in one session he could run back to where he was originally sent and confusion will set in.

In competitive obedience tests, the area the dog is sent to is very often indicated by white or other distinctive markers and the dog can soon learn to go into a marked 'box'. The method we have used to train the Sendaway means that he can actually perform a 'blind' Sendaway anywhere and not require any visible markers, but if you want to 'box'-train your dog, this is quite easy. While you are still using the mat, put the four markers around it to indicate a box area. You need do nothing else to indicate these to your dog, as he will gradually realize that this area is always where he is sent to, and he will eventually always run to an indicated box area.

You have still been walking up to your dog to finish the exercise, but when he is reliably and quickly going into the Down, the normal way to finish is by the advanced or Test A Recall. When he is down, walk towards him, about-turn in front of him, and call him to heel (as described below).

Test A Recall

The Test A Recall is so called because it is first introduced in the Test A class. Instead of leaving the dog and calling him to sit in front of you, he is actually called to heel while you are still walking away from him, and the two of you continue forward doing heelwork.

Before starting this exercise, your dog needs to be quite proficient at heelwork off the lead. As with every other exercise, you need to start with him on the lead, but in this case you will need a longer length, maybe two leads joined together or a length of nylon cord.

It is easy for a dog to start anticipating this exercise and not staying when he is told, as he will find it fun chasing after you. Guard against this by leaving him and returning to the Heel position several times without calling him. This will reinforce the Stay part of the exercise. When you are ready to call him, tell him to 'Wait', leave him and as you reach the end of the lead call his name and give the command 'Heel'. It often helps to look round to him and pat your left leg as you call him. As he comes to you, gather the lead up until it is normal length as he reaches you. Carry on for a few paces of heelwork, release and praise him.

As he gets more proficient, and you no longer need the use of a lead, make the Recall more difficult and interesting by taking several

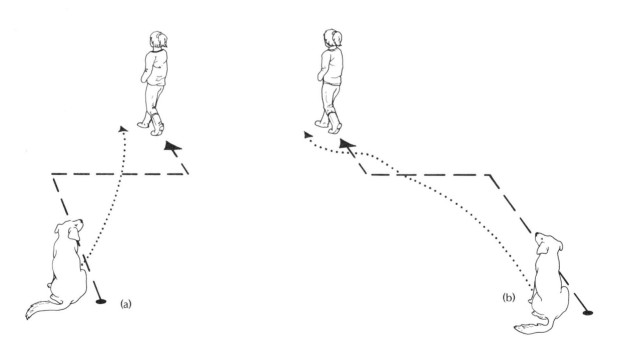

(a)   (b)

The Test 'A' Recall. (a) Initially make the recall easy by calling the dog from his right. He will then automatically join you on your left-hand side. (b) When he is more competent, call him from his left-hand side. He will then have to think about joining you in the correct heelwork position.

left, right and about-turns before calling him. Always make sure he joins your left side to continue the heelwork, and use hand signals to aid him if he gets confused when first learning the exercise.

Scent Discrimination

Scent discrimination should come naturally to any dog, as his nose is the most used of his senses and is extremely highly developed.

Book after book can be written on the theories of how dogs scent and what external factors can affect their scenting ability. The subject is vast and if you are considering progressing into serious competitive work involving scenting exercises, you really need to join an active competitive club. If, however, you are wanting to teach your dog purely for your own pleasure, read on.

Dogs are natural scenters. Just watch them on a walk, they are always following trails or using their noses to investigate things. Develop your puppy's scenting ability from a young age by encouraging him to find his favourite toy, first at home and then while you are out with him. In the park, throw his ball into long grass and let him find it.

When teaching your dog scent discrimination, that is, teaching him to differentiate one scent from another, you will need to enlist the help of a friend. Before starting the exercise, ask your helper to bring along 'irretrievable' articles that are impossible for your dog to pick up, or at least very difficult. Items such as bricks or large upturned saucepan lids are suitable. This will prevent the dog making mistakes in the early stages.

Great care has to be taken that none of these articles has the slightest trace of your scent on them. It will cause considerable confusion if you try to teach him scent when several of the articles belong to you. Even if these articles come from your home, and you

do not actually think you have handled them, there is a chance that your dog could smell something familiar on them.

Your helper should put about three of these articles on the ground and then hold your dog while you put his favourite toy amongst them. Let him see you put the article out. With your dog on the lead at your side, prepare him for the exercise. He needs to learn how to take scent. Cup your hand loosely over his nose; do not press tightly against it. As he breathes in, he will take in your scent and will learn this is the scent he is to go out and find. Tell him to 'Seek' or 'Find', but whatever command you choose, make sure you use only that one in all future training sessions. Take him, on the lead, up to the articles. Point to the irretrievable objects so that he sniffs them. When he reaches his article, he should pick it up straight away. If he does not, encourage him to do so. Praise him, run backwards out of the scent area, and then take the article.

The fact that he is not actually scenting but visually recognizing his article does not matter at this stage. All we are doing is conveying the idea to him that he has to go and find something of his own from amongst a selection of strange articles. This is why, at this early stage, you should let him see his toy being put out. If he does try to pull straight to his toy, just restrain him gently and encourage him to sniff the other articles first. When he seems to have got the idea, start hiding his article behind larger ones so that he cannot actually see it, and has to start using his nose. Gradually increase the difficulty of the exercise by using less familiar toys and by not letting him see them being put out.

The first time you use an article he is not familiar with, make sure you scent it well by rubbing it in your hands first. Go to the articles with him, getting him to sniff them, and when he reaches yours, encourage him to fetch it. It will not be long before he realizes that you are always wanting him to bring back the article with your scent on. This is why it is imperative that none of the other articles have any trace of your scent on them at all.

In obedience competition, the articles are all identical in order to avoid any chance of a dog recognizing his article by sight. Your dog should now be capable of doing this. You can also start to introduce decoys, that is articles that have your helper's scent on them rather than being left 'blank'.

Progression should only be made when you are sure the dog is absolutely confident in the stage he is currently at. Once you reach the stage of performing a scent test on identical articles that even you cannot tell apart, you have to rely implicitly on your dog. He cannot look to your for help. The most successful scent dogs are those who have been taken slowly through the stages, and have not been allowed to make mistakes and bring wrong articles back to their owners. The dog has to have absolute confidence in his abilities and not doubt himself. It is important, therefore, never to tell the dog off if he occasionally brings back the wrong article. There may be many reasons for the odd failure: he may have wind-scented your article and mistakenly picked up the one nearest to him at that time; it may be that the articles were washed in the same detergent, or a thousand other reasons. You will not know why he has failed, but if he thinks he is right, just take the article and put it down to experience. Do not try any more that day. If, however, he fails again, go back a few stages and put him back on the lead so that he is not allowed to make mistakes.

Scent discrimination is an extremely complicated exercise, and needs a lot of careful thought and study on the owner's part to avoid a dog becoming confused.

CHAPTER 12

Taking On an Older Dog

The methods so far described in this book will have enabled you to mould and train a puppy to fit into your home, happy to accept your rules and ideals. He will be biddable and able to accept commands from you because you will have established your role as leader from the very beginning.

In achieving this relationship, you will also have had to accept the problems associated with puppyhood, the house-training and possibly chewing and destructive habits. So, you may prefer the idea of rehoming an older dog who has found his way into one of the dog rescue homes or centres. However, before you take this step, you need to be fully aware of the problems associated with the idea, prior to going and actually being confronted face to face with an unwanted waif, with large appealing eyes, that you will be unable to walk away from.

Of course, it is an admirable thought to try to rehome an unwanted dog and it can be very successful. However, if you are an inexperienced dog owner, you must be fully aware of what you may be taking on. This is no reflection at all on the homes or rescue centres as they do a marvellous job, but it has to be said that a large number of dogs in rescue centres are there because they were somebody else's problem. That problem could be major: the dog might be aggressive, uncontrollable, not get on with children or have grown too big; or it could be any one of a hundred minor problems. In the majority of cases, it will not be the dog's fault that he has developed the way he has; frequently, it is the result of bad upbringing and lack of necessary care in the first few months of puppyhood, which so often happens when people buy puppies on impulse.

Having been responsible enough to read thus far, you are now aware that the two major character faults which lead to the majority of problems, aggression and nervousness, can be dealt with and eradicated if recognized early enough in a puppy's first few months. It is also these early few months that are so important in establishing the correct relationship with a dominant dog. However, if these problems have not been dealt with by the time the dog reaches adolescence, the chances are they never will be. It would take an extremely experienced dog trainer to be able to cope with them.

So, let us look at the most common reasons that dogs find their way into these homes, so that you may at least have some idea of the pitfalls to look out for, and whether you could cope with them.

First, there is the genuine, lost dog who has been found roaming and taken directly to the home. The home will, therefore, have no details about the dog's history other than what you yourself can visibly see. They will be able to give you some idea of the dog's age, whether he looked as if he had been well cared for when brought in, or looked as if he was streetwise and used to straying.

A dog who is used to straying on his own will

A dog who has found his way to a rescue centre. Was he abandoned because he has serious problems or is he a genuine case? You will probably not find out until you have kept him at home for a few months.

be very hard to reform. He will have got used to being his own boss and will certainly resent being confined in any way. It will be difficult to keep him in, as he will be a great escapologist.

Any holes in the fences will obviously be found, but he will not be afraid of jumping gates or fences to obtain his freedom. A 6-foot (1.8 m) fence can be easily scaled by a deter-

124

mined dog. The major problem, however, is that since he has always been used to being his own boss, he may get resentful when you start laying down rules and regulations on how he is to behave in your home. If the dog has been kennelled all his life, it will be very difficult for him to adapt to living within the home. He will not be used to the niceties of a comfortable living room and is likely to jump over small tables or knock ornaments flying if he feels he needs to get anywhere in a hurry. You need to establish yourself as leader, and in the early weeks this may be a real battle. This situation is dealt with in Chapter 13 under 'Dominance and Aggression' (*see* pages 126–9).

On the other hand, the genuine lost dog may be a well-mannered, well-brought-up individual that you will have no serious problems with, although the rules he had to live with in his previous home may be different to yours and require patience on your side in retraining.

The second type of dog is the one who has been brought to the home directly by his owner, so some of his history will then be known, that is, whether he has lived with children, cats or other pets, whether he is house-trained, and so on. There may be a genuine reason for the previous owner's having to part with him, emigration, family break-ups or even the owner's death. More often than not it is because the owner cannot cope for some reason: there is a new baby in the family, the dog has grown too big, or the owner cannot afford him. These are all situations that either should never have happened, or should not have necessitated the dog's rehoming when they did. These are the cases where the dog has been bought on impulse with no real thought to the responsibilities involved and, therefore, the basic puppy training has probably been sadly lacking. These owners may actually be genuinely fond of the dog and so if there are any real problems with him, for instance, snapping at children, aggression towards men, inability to become house-trained, they are unlikely to tell the home in case he does not get rehomed. They feel their conscience is cleared if they give a good report on their 'reject'.

In conclusion, it is worth remembering that even the best-behaved dog will have been living to a different set of rules to your own, and it is only after having the dog in your own home for a few weeks that you will find out all his quirks and idiosyncrasies.

CHAPTER 13

Problem Reference Sections

Refer to these sections if a persistent problem has arisen with your dog, or if you have taken on an older dog who may already have established bad habits.

There can be no magic cures and none of these problems will be cured overnight. Some dogs may take months to reform. The secret of success lies in being consistent and giving any method enough time to take effect. It is worthless trying a suggested solution for a week and then giving up saying it is ineffective. As said at the beginning of this book, dogs are creatures of habit, and once a habit is established it becomes part of a dog's character. Retraining is far more difficult than guiding a young puppy along the right lines in the first place.

Aggression

Aggressive behaviour occurs for one of three reasons: the dog is frightened, the dog is dominant or the dog is in pain. You need to establish the reason behind your dog's aggression, since the cures for each situation are very different.

If your dog is a bossy, confident type and is showing aggression in any situation, it is because he has been allowed to become the pack leader. He will act totally predictably in all the situations which confront him. He can be aggressive towards strangers entering *his* property or approaching any members of *his* pack. He can be aggressive towards members of *his* pack if they try to give him orders or challenge him in any way; a pack leader never takes or obeys orders from subordinates. He will certainly be possessive about his food and his belongings and will show aggression towards anyone, including those in his own pack, who tries to remove them from him.

He should never have been allowed to reach this position in the first place, and he has now to learn that none of these things are his by right, but only by *your* grace. There are two ways of approaching this problem, with a combination of both probably working best. He has to be ousted from the leadership position and this can be achieved either by subtle methods and a simple change of your attitude towards your dog, or, failing that, with a very dominant dog, by exercising physical strength or superiority over him, which is exactly how he would be ousted in the wild pack.

Refer to the section on dominance (*see* page 129) and immediately put into practice all the exercises mentioned. All members of the family should do this.

If any aggression is shown towards you at any time it has to be stopped immediately, no ifs and buts about it. If you back off, even once, it is reinforcing what the dog already suspects, that if he bites you, he will frighten you off and maintain his position above you. The instant you meet any resistance from the dog, quickly get hold of the scruff either side of his neck, lift his front feet from the ground, stand above him, look him straight in the eye and shake him, severely reprimanding him with a gruff, low voice. This is using language he understands. A dominant dog always grabs a submissive dog by the neck and shakes him, the dominant dog always standing above the beaten dog and growling at him. By holding the dog either side of his neck he will not be able to bite you. Be as severe as it is necessary to stop the aggression; if you do not win now, you will reinforce his superior position. When you feel the dog has submitted, push him to the ground and stand over him, only allowing him to get up when you are certain he has given up.

If the dog is aggressive with people coming to the house, you should find the situation will improve as you practise the dominance exercises and he is demoted from the position of leader. He will be able to accept more discipline from you and you should enforce the 'bed routine' already discussed in puppy training (see page 57). When people arrive, make him go to his bed and stay there until you allow him to come and greet them. If he is still inclined to show aggression to people, you need to establish yourself in a position of control, so always have him on a lead and check-chain as people arrive so that you can correct him, and prevent him from intimidating your visitors. If he does so, jerk him away, saying 'No' firmly, and put him in the Sit position.

If your dog is of a nervous or shy disposition, his aggression is a form of defence for himself, and the remedy is completely different to that described above. Refer to the sections on fear-biting and nervousness (see pages 130 and 134).

If your dog suddenly shows aggression which is completely out of character, it may be that he is in pain. First, check him over to see that he has not any sores or other external, visible problem. Check his ears and mouth to see if he resents your touching them which could indicate infections of some sort. If none are to be found, assess his general attitude: does he appear unwell or lethargic in his behaviour? When you have established as much information as you can, take him to the vet for a check-over.

If there is no medical reason for his behaviour, refer to the section on dominance (see page 129) and start the exercises as soon as possible.

Car Sickness

Make sure you do not feed your dog immediately prior to a journey in the car. Try to overcome the problem by taking the dog on very short journeys, only to somewhere he enjoys going, such as the park; have a game with him and then make the short journey home. Eventually, his anticipation of the pleasure at the end of the car journey should distract him enough from the car sickness for it not to take hold. Gradually increase the length of the journey.

Travel sickness is often caused by the dog's awareness of movement outside the car. If the problem is very bad, try travelling with him sitting on the floor in the front well of the passenger seat. This is not a satisfactory long-term arrangement, as your attention can be diverted from your driving, but as a short-term measure, it is quite often effective.

It is possible to obtain travel-sickness remedies from pet shops, but they are not always effective, and should certainly never be used as a long-term measure.

Some dogs may never get over the problem completely, and may continue to dribble profusely, which is the first sign of travel sickness. In this case, all you can do is make sure your car is protected by newspapers on the floor and take a towel with you to dry him off when you arrive at your destination.

127

Destructive Behaviour

Destructive behaviour in an adult dog is a habit that has been allowed to develop unchecked from puppyhood. Such dogs are bored (as a result of inactivity both mentally and physically) and lonely. Dogs are pack animals and need company either human or canine.

The first step to breaking the habit is to try to exercise your dog and go through some training exercises before leaving him. He will probably sleep for a short period after this and if you try not to leave him too long, you will return to him before he has performed any destructive act. If you have to leave him for longer periods, make sure you leave some-

Consider using an indoor kennel if your dog is really destructive when left. Make sure you exercise him before leaving him.

thing interesting for him to chew on, such as a large marrow bone, and leave a lot of his own toys with him. If you suspect your dog will be destructive when you leave him, it is up to you to make sure you remove all your treasures such as your best shoes, handbags and so on.

If this does not work, there is no point telling him off when you return home. He will not know what you are cross for; he will not associate it with an act he did a few hours ago. If the problem persists you will need to catch him in the act. Deliberately leave something in the room that you know he will chew on. Then, follow the same routine you would normally adopt when going out, picking up keys, putting on your coat, but do not actually leave the house. Go to another room and wait and listen. As soon as you hear him start to chew, you can spring in, surprise him and reprimand him instantly.

If he really is determined, and all else fails, you may need to consider using an indoor kennel for him, at least for a few months until the habit is broken. There are various types of indoor kennel, from all-wire types to more enclosed travelling-type cages. Make sure you choose one of a suitable size. Once you have prevented him from being destructive for a few months, it will not occur to him to do so – the bad habit will have been eradicated. If you are using an indoor kennel, ensure that he has his water bowl in the kennel with him, and also his own toys. It is also a good idea to leave a radio playing softly, as this will help to prevent his feeling lonely or bored. Finally, it is only fair to exercise the dog first and not to leave him confined all day. Somebody should at least go and exercise him at lunchtime.

Disobedience towards One Member of the Family

This is yet another problem associated with the pack behaviour of the dog, and dominance. A dog will obey anybody in the family whom he considers superior to himself. The usual situation is that the dog obeys the man of the house, while the lady, who probably tends to all the dog's needs including feeding and letting him in and out, can do nothing with the dog all day. The dog obeys the man because he respects him.

Anyone who is being ignored by the dog needs to put into practice all the exercises referred to in the section on dominance (*see* below).

Dogs in the Same House not Getting On

If two dogs living together are left to their own devices, they will co-exist quite happily. They will establish their pack order quite quickly and a top dog and a underdog will emerge. Once these roles are established, both parties will be content with the situation. Problems arise because of human interference during this period of adjustment, and because the outcome might not seem to us and our human values a fair one.

When we introduce a young puppy into our house with an existing older dog, we expect the old dog to maintain his top position in the house. Unfortunately, this rarely happens because, as the younger, fitter dog grows up, he will expect to take over as boss dog. A problem occurs if the older dog is not prepared to give up his place. The situation is normally sorted out by a show of strength followed by a fight. Usually, no real damage is inflicted and, if the dogs are left to sort it out, the problem is solved there and then. When he knows he is beaten in a fight, the underdog will adopt a submissive posture (he will lie on the floor), and both dogs will usually just walk away. Unfortunately, though, many owners will interfere and are inclined to side with the older dog, which is the wrong thing to do

because it will only keep the bad feeling between the two simmering on for months and months. However, if an older dog is being particularly aggressive towards a puppy, the puppy will obviously need protection from you until he is old enough to look after himself. This is not a common occurrence, but, in the event, the two dogs should never be left alone together.

The owner and all other members of the family must be dominant over both dogs. The dog who is emerging as top dog must then have his position continually reinforced over the weaker dog. He must be fed first, given any treats first, greeted first and given privileges above the other dog. It does not seem very fair in our eyes, but once the positions are established, the dogs will be perfectly happy to accept them. They are unhappy and confused if they are not allowed to establish their roles in relation to each other. We cannot decide who we want to be top dog; they have to sort it out themselves and we must back up the eventual outcome. Once again, problems only arise with dominant dogs. Submissive dogs make no demands at all, and are quite happy to be on the bottom rung of the ladder.

Dominance

The single, biggest reason why dogs are branded as 'problem dogs' is that the pack hierarchy has not been established correctly in your own home. The dog who has been allowed to become top dog over all other members of the family is disobedient, defiant, often bossy to the point of aggression, or even downright nasty. He makes his own rules, decides who is to visit *his* property or who is to be seen off. This is, of course, a totally unacceptable situation in our society and he has to be demoted. In the wild, the pack leader is usually overcome by the sheer superior physical strength and cunning of a younger, more powerful, ambitious youngster. As a last resort, physical strength may be needed in order to dominate your dog, but first try to establish your leadership in more subtle ways, by trying the following exercises. The most important point to remember is that you must never jump to demands made by your dog:

1. When your dog comes and nudges you for a fuss, do not respond. Tell him to lie down or go to his bed. Call him to you a few minutes later and fuss him. When you arrive home, ignore your dog and make him go to his bed. Call him to you when you are in and settled. It is the pack leader who demands or gives attention when he wants it, on his terms. You must put yourself in that position.

2. Prepare your dog's food, put it aside and have your dinner first. Do not let him beg titbits from the table. The pack leader always eats first; the subordinate members of the pack eat last.

3. If he goes to the door demanding to be let into the garden, do not jump up to do so. Tell him to lie down or go to his bed. Let him out when you decide to allow him out a few minutes later. (Obviously this can only be put into practice with an adult dog, and not with a puppy that you are still trying to house-train. Do not do this if you know your dog has a tummy upset.)

4. If your dog is lying asleep indoors and you want to pass, do not step round or over him. Make him move out of your way. It is only a pack leader who can expect this deference from others.

5. When going out, never let the dog pass through the door before you. The pack leader always leads from the front, going ahead of subordinates. Make sure this leader is you. Tell the dog to wait, or even to sit and stay until you are through the door and then let him follow behind.

6. Never let the dog sleep on your bed or get on the furniture. The pack leader sleeps in the best places on a higher level than the rest of the pack. Your dog must sleep in his bed on the floor.

In all of the above situations, you have put yourself in the dominant role. Your dog should become generally more obedient as he comes to accept your leadership, and will then be prepared to take orders from you.

In the case of a very dominant dog who has been allowed to have his own way for a long time, more drastic action may be needed. Again, look to how dogs behave in the wild. A dominant dog grabs a challenger by the scruff of the neck, shaking him and growling, until eventually the beaten dog lies on the ground with the victor standing above him. This is exactly what you must do. Any signs of aggression (the ultimate form of dominance) must be stopped. Grab the dog either side of his neck by the scruff, lift his front feet from the ground and shake him, looking him straight in the eye and scolding him severely. Before letting go, but when you feel the dog is submitting, push him to the ground, forcing his head down while you are standing above him. Only let go when you are confident that the dog has given up. You must win this battle to have any hope of reforming an aggressive, dominant dog.

Fear-Biting

A fear-biter is a very dangerous animal because it is so unpredictable and its general behaviour can be so erratic. This type of aggression is used as a last resort by a very frightened animal, who will use its teeth as its last form of defence.

If your dog is getting the upper hand you need physically to exert your dominance over him. Take him by the scruff at either side of his neck, push him to the ground and hold him down, standing over him, just as a dominant dog would do. Only when you feel he has submitted can you let him get up. Put him into the Sit, and then release him. Compare your actions with those of the dominant dog on page 37.

First, refer to and read the section on nervousness because a fear-biter is basically a nervous dog who has not been socialized properly as a puppy. As with all nervous dogs, the fear-biter has to be gradually exposed to the object or situation that is causing the problem (in this case the approach of people), be rewarded, and the level of exposure gradually increased.

Your dog has to learn that people are not going to hurt him, and to do this, you are going to need the help of some friends, preferably people who are comfortable with and not afraid of dogs. You will need to have your dog on a lead when you start to retrain him, because although punishment as such is inappropriate (we are trying to build his confidence), he obviously has to learn that he is not allowed to bite, so you need to be in a position of control.

With your dog on the lead at your side, have a friend approach you but not make any move towards touching your dog. If he tries to back off or growl, keep him in position and tell him

131

'No', but at the same time stroke him confidently to try to get across to him that there is nothing to fear. When the dog is quite happy to let the person approach, he can then try to bend down and stroke the dog. This should be attempted only when you feel the dog has enough confidence to be able to cope with it. Obviously, this progress should be made over a period of time; do not try to reform your dog in one session.

Any growling or resentment has to be firmly stopped, while remembering all the time that you need to build his confidence. The person should offer the dog one of his favourite titbits and eventually he will learn that strangers can be friends. Always make sure the person bends down to the dog's level and never towers above him, reaching down, since this is very intimidating to a nervous dog and threatening to an aggressive dog.

A fear-biter will never be 100 per cent reliable with strangers, although with careful training he should turn out to be a dog you can live with. However, you must always be on guard for the unexpected, say, people rushing up to him in a strange place. If he is cornered he will bite out of fear to defend himself.

Fighting with Other Dogs

If your dog is aggressive towards other dogs, it indicates either that he has not been socialized properly as a puppy, or that he was taken from his mother and litter-mates too early and now has difficulty in relating to his own kind.

A course at a dog-training school should help as he will be gradually introduced to other dogs in a confined space. Your dog should be on a lead and a check-chain at all times and if a dog approaches and your dog responds by growling or raising his hackles, jerk him back saying 'No' very firmly. Put him in the Sit position so you retain control. You will have to be as firm as is necessary to stop the aggression. Do not force the situation and, only gradually, perhaps over a period of days or weeks, allow the other dogs to come closer.

When you are out and you know your dog is still inclined to be aggressive to other dogs, you need to be constantly alert and try to avoid any unsupervised meeting. The more times your dog is allowed to fight and win, the more he will learn to enjoy it. Fighting with other dogs is, again, a sign of dominance. The best thing that could happen to your dog would be for him to meet another aggressive, more powerful dog who would beat him, but although this is what would happen in the wild, it is obviously not an acceptable solution to see enacted in our suburban parks. The slow-approach method above has to be used.

If, however, a fight does break out, the best thing to do, in the vast majority of cases, is to let the dogs sort it out themselves. They will not actually fight on to cause any serious injury, and one dog will usually submit and lie on the floor. Although there will be a lot of noise, both dogs will usually walk away unharmed. Any screaming and shouting by the owners will usually only inflame the situation. The only time you should interfere is if a fight is particularly one-sided, the aggressor is particularly aggressive and still carries on fighting after the weaker dog has submitted. This is *not* a common occurrence. If water is available via a bucket or hose, direct it at the dogs. This will usually distract their attention for long enough for you to be able to get hold of their collars. Once you have hold of the collar, twist it so that it tightens round the dog's neck causing the dog to let go in order to breathe. Put into practice all the exercises in the section on dominance (*see* page 129).

General Disobedience

Refer to the section on dominance (*see* page 129).

House-Training

Establish first whether your expectations are too great for the dog's age. Are you leaving him too long? Sometimes a change in the feeding routine can solve the problem. If you are feeding just one large meal, change to offering two smaller meals and then experiment with the times of feeding. Always check that when the dog is let out, either last thing at night or just before you leave him during the day he does actually relieve himself. It may help if you walk round with him to encourage him. If, after these changes, there is no improvement, take him to the vet to check there is nothing medically wrong with him.

If he is pronounced healthy, is of an age to be able to hold himself for reasonable periods, has been trained correctly, and there is still a problem, remedial action needs to be started as soon as possible, because the dog is now in the habit of being dirty when left and the longer it carries on, the harder it will be to cure. No healthy animal will foul his bed, so you need to be able to confine him in such a way that he is only able to sleep in his bed area, while obviously being allowed at least to turn around and get comfortable.

One method is to tie him to an immovable object near to his bed. The lead needs to be long enough for him to be able to lie down and turn around. Do not leave a dog tied with a check-chain on in case the lead should become caught in any way, although obviously you will take precautions to make sure there is nothing for it to get caught on. Always leave him attached with a fixed, leather collar. Alternatively, you could confine him by using one of the indoor kennels now available from pet stores or, in the case of smaller dogs, a box with sides high enough to keep him in.

This method should only be needed on a temporary basis (say, a couple of months) until the habit is broken. Before leaving the dog confined, make sure he is exercised and has relieved himself first. He should not be left all day, somebody should return to him at lunchtime. There is no problem leaving him all night. You must confine him each and every time he is left, as it is the only way to break the habit and start a new one, and this must be done for at least a couple of months before you try to leave him free again. You must be sure the old habit is completely eradicated.

If, when confined to his bed area, the dog is still dirty, it indicates that he is either too young to hold himself for long periods, or that there is a physical or mental problem with him. In these cases, it may be that the only answer would be to have him kennelled outside. However, a dog who is too young to hold himself should not be left for long periods, anyway, and a dog who has a physical problem should be treated by the vet.

Jumping Up

Once established, this habit can be very hard to cure because of the sheer excitement being generated at the time of the misdemeanour, usually when you are being greeted after being away for a time. Any pushing, shouting and waving about of arms only inflame the situation more, as the dog thinks he is having a great game with you. There are several methods that can be tried to eliminate the problem.

Never ever greet your dog when you come home, walk in and completely ignore him. This may seem a strange thing to say, but in fact it is very practical. It can be more than a nuisance when you arrive home laden with carrier bags of shopping and you have to try to force your way past the dog. There can be tears if you arrive home after picking up young children from school, who can get knocked over in the rush. If you never greet your dog as you enter the house, he will accept this and not think about rushing to see you. He will lie in his bed until you are ready to call him to you. Refer to the section on dominance (*see* page 129) to understand the further implications of this.

If the situation persists, push him down very firmly and deliberately, putting your hands on his shoulders. Give the command 'No'. Put him in the Sit, bend down to his level to greet him, to avoid the need for him to jump up. All your movements should be slow and deliberate to avoid more excitement. When you arrive home, tell him to find 'Ball' or some other favourite toy. This will send him off hunting, giving you the chance to get in and greet him properly, bending down to his level.

If jumping up at visitors is the problem, use the bed routine explained in the puppy training section (*see* page 57). Always make him go to his bed and stay there while you let people in. Only call him when everybody is settled. The personal alarm deterrent is also effective in curing a dog who jumps up (*see* page 43).

If the problem is really difficult and none of the above methods work, you may need to try the following. As the dog rushes to you and is about to jump up, lift your right leg so that as he jumps he is pushed backwards off balance. Timing is critical and you may need a few attempts to get it right. Immediately afterwards, bend down quickly to his level and praise him.

Jumping up is another sign of dominance and the exercises described in the section on dominance should be read and put into practice (*see* page 129).

Nervousness

A nervous dog is a very unhappy dog, who lives in constant fear of unexpected noises or situations. He is not usually fun to own as his fear of the world prevents him from being able to offer much to you, and the relationship is very one-sided, you being the one offering constant support and back-up. Even your regular walks to the park can be a terrifying experience for a very nervous dog.

The tragedy is that if the problem is recognized early enough during the puppy's formative weeks, socializing and conditioning can at least enable the adult dog to cope with his nervousness and learn to live with his anxieties. Life can then be more acceptable and fun for both of you. However, overcoming nervousness in an adult dog is a painstaking, tedious business requiring infinite patience from the owner. Any signs of short temper or impatience on the owner's part can set the training back months.

First, establish whether there are any specific things the dog is particularly averse to, and start working on these areas. If the dog is nervous of people, refer also to the section on fear-biting (*see* page 130).

An object that commonly puts fear into even a slightly apprehensive dog is the vacuum cleaner, a big noisy monster that appears to chase after things on the floor and gobble them up. The method of getting a dog to accept that this object is not going to hurt or attack him in any way will work for any situation your dog is frightened of.

The dog has to be made to face up to his fear very, very slowly and in small doses at a time. The situation will only be made worse if you think he is just being silly, and force him up to something that frightens him. For instance, in the case of a dog who is frightened of traffic, it is no help at all if you plunge him into the middle of a busy high street with huge lorries thundering up and down.

In the case of the vacuum cleaner, start by just showing the dog the cleaner while it is switched off. Encourage him towards it, and praise him. Offer him a titbit when he is there. Only when he is completely comfortable with the cleaner when it is switched off can you proceed to the next stage (in the meantime you will have to make sure that your dog is always in another room when you are doing the housework).

Next, you need to have someone to help you. With the cleaner one end of the room and you and your dog the other, get your friend to switch it on. When this happens, try to have your dog's attention on you by playing with him. If the dog is startled, try to encourage him to carry on with the game, but if he cannot, just reassure him. There is a fine line between giving him confidence and making him feel there is really something to be fearful of, so although you need to praise him, do not sympathize with him. The process continues day by day, or in bad cases, week by week, until you reach the stage where you can start taking him nearer to the dreaded object. Only progress as far as he is capable of at any time and do not force the issue on him. Of course, you must make sure that at no time during the training is the cleaner switched on close to him by accident by anyone in the house, because if he is startled at this stage, it will undo all the progress you have made.

If it is not specific objects that frighten him, but certain situations that he finds himself in, the remedy is similar. Gradually build up his level of exposure to the object of fear. If he is frightened of traffic or walking along the streets, take him first to a very quiet side road where you know only the occasional car passes. Walk up and down and, as a car approaches, try to distract his attention from it by playing with him. If he really is too frightened to be able to carry on, fuss him and praise him, acting confidently yourself. Gradually get him used to busier roads and heavier traffic.

A nervous dog will restrict you in many ways, especially while you are retraining him, when every move has to be very carefully thought out by you. If you can make his world a less fearful place for him, then all the hard work really is worth it.

New Baby in the House

Provided your dog has been well socialized and brought up in a fairly disciplined way, there should be absolutely no problems when a new baby arrives in the home. Your dog poses no health risk to the baby if he is wormed regularly (every six months) and if he is not allowed to lick the baby's face. Assuming that you knew there was the possibility of a new addition to the household within the dog's life span, you would have been careful, when acquiring your puppy, to choose a suitable breed. You are also prepared to accept that dogs and babies can co-exist or you would not have acquired the dog in the first place.

When a new baby arrives, there are new rules that the dog is going to have to learn to accept, but, providing you are sensible, these should not cause any resentment from the dog. Jealousy will only occur if the situation is not handled sensibly.

When the baby arrives home, the dog will be curious and you should allow him to see the new arrival. Overbearing behaviour on your part at this stage can be the start of a jealousy problem arising. If the dog attempts to lick the baby he should be told firmly 'No', pulled back by his collar and then praised for responding. Do not isolate the dog; let him sit with you when you are holding the baby. Never, though, leave a dog alone with a young baby. If you leave the room, take one or the other with you.

When the baby cries, the dog is bound to be curious and will naturally go to the baby to see what is wrong. There should be no over-reaction on your part, but careful supervision. If the dog is going too close, tell him 'No' firmly.

If your dog is generally disobedient and boisterous, refer to the section on dominance and implement the suggestions to give you more general control. When the baby is asleep, give the dog extra attention and fuss.

Common sense must prevail when you leave children with dogs. In this picture, it appears the owner has left his dog attached to the pushchair and there is no adult nearby supervising. This dog may be 100 per cent reliable, but what if an aggressive dog approached and attacked him? The pushchair would be pulled over and in the ensuing chaos, the child has every chance of being bitten.

Do not ignore the dog and forget his requirements and routines either.

If your dog is a nervous fear-biter or has been allowed to develop into an individual with aggressive tendencies, then obviously, serious thought will have to be given as to the wisdom of trying to allow the baby and the dog to co-exist in the same house. You will have to be extra vigilant at all times and this may be a situation where rehoming might be con-sidered. Contact breed rescue societies where possible, but be absolutely honest with them in your reasons for parting with your dog and your assessment of his character.

Noisiness

Noisy dogs are notoriously difficult to cure once the problem is established because they are usually only noisy when you have left them. You are not then in a position to correct them. However, correct them you must, or you are no doubt going to fall out with everybody in the neighbourhood.

You are going to need to set up the situation and leave your dog when you know he is going to bark. Leave the house but do not actually go away. As soon as he starts to bark, quickly open the door telling him 'Quiet' in a severe voice. Leave him in no doubt as to the error of his ways by the look on your face and your tone of voice. It is inappropriate to punish him physically; it will serve no purpose in this situation.

Repeat this several times, leaving and returning to him if he barks. You will need the help of your neighbour as it may be that he is not noisy all the time, but only at certain times, for instance, when people pass the house. If you live in a quiet road, this is no problem as all dogs are allowed to bark occasionally during your absence, but if you are on a busy road and the barking is becoming incessant, you will again need someone's help. Ask your helper to walk past your house so that you can then correct your dog as soon as he starts to bark. Alternatively, a simpler solution may be to confine him to a back room when you leave him, thus removing the cause of his barking.

If your returning and scolding him does not prove to be effective, try the personal alarm deterrent. As your dog barks, open the letter-box, say 'Quiet' and, if he does not respond, activate the alarm. This is a method your neighbour could use to help you overcome the problem when you are out for a period of time. If each time he starts to bark, your neighbour uses the alarm through the letter-box, or near an open window, the dog should soon learn to be quiet. Of course, while this training is going on, always make sure your dog has something to interest him while you are out. Refer to the section on destructive behaviour (*see* page 128) as many of the ideas used there are also related to this problem.

The problem of noisiness in cars is difficult to overcome for two reasons. First, the dog soon learns that you are powerless to do anything while you are behind the wheel of the car and, second, the problem is a result of sheer excitement and the more you shout at him the worse he will get. In very bad cases the noise of the car's indicators can send him into a near frenzy as he thinks he has reached his destination.

There are several methods you can try to ease the situation. The dog is noisy because he associates travelling in the car with going somewhere exciting, usually to the park or woods. Take him on some dummy runs in the car, perhaps when you are going shopping or to visit friends, and leave him in the car. Only let him out when you get home. Sit in the car when it is stationary and put the indicators on to accustom him to them when he is in a calmer mood and more likely to hear your reprimand. *On no account, leave a dog in a car for even a short time on a hot day*, so you will need to be careful and choose suitable days. Even with the windows open the temperature in a stationary car soars. It is extremely cruel and is often fatal. While you are trying this 'dummy run' method, you will need to walk your dog locally so that there is no need for you to take him in the car to his favourite place. He needs to learn that every trip in the car will be boring.

You may need to enlist the help of a friend who could sit on the back seat and physically reprimand the dog to stop him barking on your

command 'Quiet'. This is not always effective because he will know that when you are on your own you are again helpless to do anything.

One of the most effective methods is the use of the personal alarm. Tell the dog 'Quiet' and, if he does not respond, activate the alarm. The advantage is that he will not know where the noise has come from, only that if he does not respond to your command, this dreadful ear-piercing noise starts. He will not necessarily associate it with you. Praise him when he goes quiet.

Pulling on Lead

A dog who pulls on the lead is showing dominant tendencies: he is trying always to go ahead to lead the pack. First, refer to the section on dominance (*see* page 129). In addition, the following specific actions will help.

If the dog is still on a fixed collar, change to a check-chain type of collar, learn the correct way of using it and do ten minutes heelwork training per day in the park.

Do not walk him along the streets to the park or along any route that he is familiar with, otherwise he will be more single-minded in reaching his destination and you will be fighting an uphill battle in getting him to listen to you.

When walking along the street, keep changing direction. As he passes you to get in front, give a quick jerk with the chain to off-balance him, and then keep his attention on you by holding a titbit or one of his favourite playthings, remembering to praise him when he responds correctly.

Over-Sexed Dogs

A dog who tries to mount and mate with your leg or a visitor's leg is highly embarrassing. It is, of course, unacceptable behaviour that is far more common in male dogs, although younger bitches can go through the phase.

Very often such dogs will grow out of it as they mature, but they must be taught that it is wrong from the very beginning, and it has to be stopped. The dog is usually aroused by excitement, which is why it often happens when visitors arrive. So, you should avoid any further excitement, such as shouting, pushing the dog away or trying to shake him off the leg, which will only encourage him more.

Be very deliberate in your actions: take him by the scruff at the back of his neck, pull him off and tell him 'No' firmly. Put him in the Down position to put yourself back in the situation of control, or send him to his bed.

Some of the larger, guarding breeds take longer to mature than other dogs, but eventually they should grow out of it. If the problem is really persistent you may need to discuss the possibility of castration with your vet.

Thieving

It is quite natural for dogs to help themselves to any food that may be within reach because they have no understanding of the moral concept of theft. Food is for eating. So, they have to be taught that they are not to help themselves in our homes.

A dog who is only fed at his own mealtimes and never given titbits at other times is less likely to steal than a dog who regularly has extras (provided, of course, that he is not being underfed). The first step with a dog that is a thief is to stop giving him any titbits at all; only feed him at a regular time with his own dinner. Making it a regular time is important, as once he is used to this time he will only expect food then, and is not likely to look for it any earlier than this. All the family must be involved and know the reasons for your enforcing this rule.

During this retraining period, make sure that food is not left around, especially when you are out. Start correction exercises. Put some food on a low table or easily accessible place and tell him to 'Leave'. If he goes to take the food, jerk him back saying 'No' firmly. Do not let him sit and drool over the food. Make him go and lie down elsewhere. Keep the food out all the time you are able to keep your eye on it, and able to correct him each time he approaches it. When you have to do other things, remove the food out of harm's way. It is easier to start this training soon after he has been fed, so that he is not actually hungry.

If the dog always raids the rubbish bin while you are out, similar tactics are employed. The dog has to be taught that the bin is out of bounds to him. When retraining starts, make sure you do not leave temptation in his way. Remove the bin from the room. Start training him by having the bin open while you are in the kitchen working. Each time he goes to it, tell him 'No' in no uncertain terms. The personal alarm is an excellent deterrent as it can be activated by you as he approaches the bin, without any apparent intervention from you at all. These 'magic' surprise reprimands always work best.

Useful Addresses

The following are the addresses of organizations and publications mentioned in the text.

The Kennel Club
1–4, Clarges Street
London
W1Y 8AB

The Kennel Club is the governing body for registration of pedigree dogs and shows. It provides lists of dog training clubs, breed societies and breeders, and registration forms for crossbreeds to enter Obedience Shows.

Pro-Dogs
4, New Road
Ditton
Kent
ME20 7AD

Pro-Dogs is a charity set up to promote responsible dog ownership. It operates the P.A.T. dog scheme. It organizes regular functions and publishes a newsletter for its members.

Dog Training Weekly
Penrhiw Cilau
Letterston
Haverfordwest
Pembrokeshire

This is the weekly journal for Obedience Competition enthusiasts, giving details of shows and judges' reports.

Dog World
9, Tufton Street
Ashford
Kent
TN23 1QN

Our Dogs
5, Oxford Road
Station Approach
Manchester
M60 1SX

Both the above publications are weekly papers for breed showing enthusiasts. They contain advertisements for puppies, breeders, shows, dog equipment, etc.

Index

(Note: Page numbers referring to illustrations appear in italics.)

INDEX

INDEX